FOCUS ON
CURVES AND
SURFACES

PREMIER PRESS

GAME DEVELOPMENT

FOCUS ON CURVES AND SURFACES

Kelly Dempski

PREMIER PRESS

GAME DEVELOPMENT

Premier
Press

The Premier Press logo and related trade dress are trademarks of Premier Press and may not be used without written permission.

Publisher: Stacy L. Hiquet

Marketing Manager: Heather Hurley

Acquisitions Editor: Mitzi Foster Koontz

Series Editor: André LaMothe

Project Editor/Copy Editor: Jenny Davidson

Technical Reviewer: Wolfgang Engel/André LaMothe

Interior Layout: Danielle Foster

Cover Designer: Mike Tanamachi

Indexer: Katherine Stimson

Proofreader: Sandi Wilson

Xfrog is a registered trademark of greenworks organic-software.

Rhino is a registered trademark of Robert McNeel & Associates.

DirectX is a registered trademark of Microsoft Corporation in the United States and/or other countries.

Adobe, the Adobe logo, Acrobat, the Acrobat logo, and Acrobat Reader are registered trademarks of Adobe Systems Incorporated in the United States and/or other countries.

All other trademarks are the property of their respective owners.

Important: Premier Press cannot provide software support. Please contact the appropriate software manufacturer's technical support line or Web site for assistance.

Premier Press and the author have attempted throughout this book to distinguish proprietary trademarks from descriptive terms by following the capitalization style used by the manufacturer.

Information contained in this book has been obtained by Premier Press from sources believed to be reliable. However, because of the possibility of human or mechanical error by our sources, Premier Press, or others, the Publisher does not guarantee the accuracy, adequacy, or completeness of any information and is not responsible for any errors or omissions or the results obtained from use of such information. Readers should be particularly aware of the fact that the Internet is an ever-changing entity. Some facts may have changed since this book went to press.

ISBN: 1-59200-007-X
Library of Congress Catalog Card Number: 2002111225
Printed in the United States of America

03 04 05 06 07 BH 10 9 8 7 6 5 4 3 2 1

Premier Press, a division of Course Technology
2645 Erie Avenue, Suite 41
Cincinnati, Ohio 45208

To my Mother and Father

Acknowledgments

T hanks to my wife, Rachel. She has endured months of incredibly stimulating conversation about knot vectors and basis functions. I have a great appreciation for her patience, and this book would not have been possible without her support.

Thanks to my family for reasons too numerous to mention.

As always, many thanks again to my friends and colleagues Scott Kurth and Mitu Singh for their time spent proofreading, offering suggestions, and providing general moral support. For that, I consider myself extremely fortunate.

Thanks to everyone at Accenture Technology Labs for their support and encouragement. I have the pleasure to work with a group of extremely intelligent and thoughtful people.

Also, I'd like to thank all of the other people who worked on this book. I really appreciate the help of Mitzi Foster, Jenny Davidson, and many others. They are extremely supportive and tolerant of strange, longwinded e-mails. Many thanks go to Wolfgang Engel for his thoughtful and thorough technical editing.

I'd also like to thank the numerous people who have contributed to this field. Without their inventions, contributions, and insight, this book would quite literally have not been possible. It would be impossible to list all of the people who have explicitly or implicitly contributed to this field, but I have included a short bibliography in Appendix C that should serve to introduce you to their work.

Finally, I'd like to thank Ben, Tom, and Will at Bagel Art (highly recommended if you are ever in Evanston, IL), and Shaun, Máire, Ian, and all the people at Starbucks (highly recommended if you are ever on Earth).

All of the people mentioned above contributed in some way to the better aspects of this book. I deeply appreciate their contributions.

About the Author

KELLY DEMPSKI has been a researcher at Accenture Technology Labs for the past eight years. His research work has been in the areas of multimedia, Virtual Reality, Augmented Reality, and Interactive TV. He has authored several papers in these areas and is also the author of *Real-Time Rendering Tricks and Techniques in DirectX* by Premier Press.

Contents at a Glance

Contents

Part One
Focus on Basics 1

Part Two
Focus on Curves 33

Letter from the Series Editor

Ever since the world saw the undulating organic geometry in id Software's *Quake III*, everyone has been trying to add this powerful technique to their games. Both OpenGL and DirectX support higher-order surfaces, but it can be difficult to use them effectively. The real root of the problem is that this technology is mathematical in nature. It's not rocket science, but it's hard to use a "rational basis spline" when you don't know what those words mean.

With that in mind, my vision for this book was something that you can pick up and walk away with knowing exactly how to create 2D/3D curves and surfaces. The problem with this book is that you need someone who is a Jedi to write it; this material is complex, and only someone with years of experience in game programming, and years of experience in this area could pull it off—luckily for us, Kelly Dempski showed up with a proposal for this book that was exactly what I was looking for.

I am constantly saying how good all these Premier *Game Development* books are, and I am going to once again. This is the world's best book on the subject, hands down. There is simply nothing that is going to give you the information in an informal, but strict, fun, but serious way that balances what you need to know with the constraints of needing to know it within your lifetime <BG>.

I just finished reviewing the final text and demo of the book, and I have to say I am amazed… The book starts off with an introduction about curves and surfaces, so you know what to expect, then Kelly (very wisely) creates a simple application framework to render curves and surfaces in a uniform manner (believe me when you start writing 50-100 demos for something, you want to be able to do it quickly). Once you have the tools to get started, then "it's on". Bezier curves are first up (being that I am French, I appreciate this of course), then B-splines (their close neighbors), and on to NURBS and subdivision curves. After all these topics have been covered, then it's round two with the 3D version of everything, and surfaces are also covered. So the transition is smooth and consistent with just enough math to get the job done, and there's a really nice calculus and vector review in the appendixes if you're a little rusty.

Finally, the book ends with some more advanced topics and delves into using DirectX 8.1+ to do all the math for us (for the most part), but like Kelly, I believe that you should know how to do this stuff—one day you might have to derive it all yourself!

In conclusion, this book rocks, and you have to have it. All the Internet articles in the world aren't going to give you what you will read in this book and immediately be able to leverage in your own work.

Sincerely,

André LaMothe
Premier *Game Development* Series Editor

Introduction

I have several graphics and geometry books on my shelf. Some of these books are very good and their authors are extremely knowledgeable. However, some of the best books are often the hardest to read. In some cases, you need to have a fairly deep understanding of the topics to even begin to grasp the new material. This book is a little different because it is based on the assumption that you are relatively new to the concepts and mathematics of curves and surfaces. I will explain the math in simple terms, with an emphasis on clarity over rigorous math. If you choose to pursue advanced topics, this book will serve as a good warm-up.

Who Is This Book For?

This book is aimed at anyone interested in learning the basic concepts behind curves and surfaces. Much of the focus is on game development, but the ideas also have applications for people who are interested in CAD, 3D modeling, and visualization. If you are working in these areas and have not had formal training in curves and surfaces, this book is for you.

How Should This Book Be Read?

There are three main parts of this book. The first part introduces the basic concepts. The second part covers curves, and the third part covers surfaces. Each part walks you through the material, starting with the basics and ending with more complex concepts. You may want to read it linearly, covering all the curve material before moving on to surfaces. You might also want to jump back and forth between the curve and surface sections. For instance, you may want to read about Bezier curves and then skip to Bezier surfaces before moving to a new topic. The choice is up to you.

Personally, I have a hard time understanding something unless I can actually see it working. Each chapter is accompanied by code that demonstrates the ideas. Also, in many cases, it might be very helpful to sketch some rough curves on graph paper. The ideas become much easier to understand when you can see them working.

What's Included

This book includes a CD of all the source code used in this book. In many cases, the figures in this book were produced by the application. If there are figures you don't understand, check to see if you can reproduce the figure using the code from the CD.

Who Am I?

I am a researcher with Accenture Technology Labs. My most recent projects have involved work in Augmented and Virtual Reality, and many other projects involving gaming consoles and very realistic graphics. I'm not a game programmer, but a large part of my work involves using and understanding the same technologies. Unlike many other authors of advanced books, I do not have a background in pure mathematics or computer science. My background is in engineering. From that perspective, my focus will be more on implementing techniques and getting things done rather than theoretical musings. If you have questions, you know where to reach me!

Thanks,

Kelly Dempski
Graphics_Book@hotmail.com

PART ONE

FOCUS ON BASICS

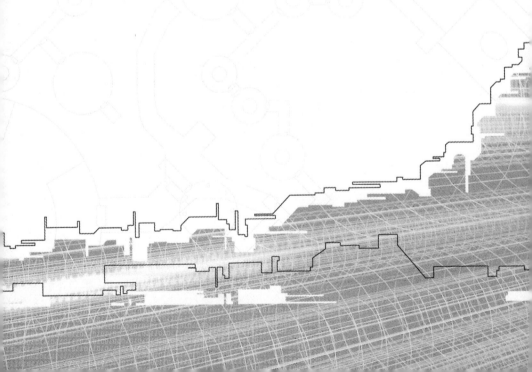

The curves and surfaces in this book are based on some fairly complex mathematics, so I've decided to begin with two chapters that briefly lay the mathematical foundation for some of the later ideas. I expect this will be review for many people, and many of the more knowledgeable people will notice that there are areas where I only skim the surface.

If you are already comfortable with trigonometry and calculus, you can probably skip these first few chapters. However, I suggest skimming them just to get a feel for how I present things.

If these concepts are new to you, read these first two chapters and the appendixes. They will definitely help in understanding the rest of the book. As you read, remember that I am giving you the pieces that you need to understand a handful of concepts, but these are by no means complete explanations of algebra, trigonometry, and calculus. That would require several books of this size. To dig deeper into the math, I strongly suggest college-level courses in calculus and beyond.

CHAPTER 1

POLYNOMIAL CURVES

A ll of the curves and surfaces in this book are based on sets of equations of varying complexity. Most of those equations are polynomial equations. In this first chapter, I will establish a mathematical and conceptual foundation for most of the chapters to follow. For those of you who've had some higher math courses, most of this should be review. For others, this will introduce you to the basics that provide an undercurrent to nearly every other chapter. I'll start off with the following points.

- What is a curve?
- What is a polynomial?
- Lines (first-degree polynomials) and slopes
- Curves (higher-degree polynomials) and derivatives
- Joining curves and continuity
- An introduction to a curve application

What Is a Curve?

I should get this out of the way as soon as possible. This is a book about curves (and surfaces), so it would be quite improper to go too much farther without first defining exactly what a curve is.

Definition

A *curve* is defined as a plot of the results of a function in space.

Now, keep in mind that this definition isn't entirely correct from a strict mathematical perspective. Because of this, I will probably never be invited to swanky mathematician dinner parties. We all must make sacrifices. A strict mathematical definition could have filled an entire chapter and this is a fairly short book.

Instead, my definition of a curve will be good enough for our purposes. In short, I am defining a curve as a plot and vice versa.

Having said that, keep in mind that the idea of a "plot" can encompass much more than something that you'd draw on a screen or a piece of paper. Imagine a car; obviously, you can think of the outline of the body as a curve, but don't forget that the motion of the car follows a curve, the fuel consumption follows a curve, and much more.

Most of the examples in this book are focused on curves and surfaces as geometric and visible graphs because visual examples are very helpful and because curves can be quite useful in the visual space. Don't let that lull you into a single mindset. Remember that curves can be used to represent so much more. This is one of the reasons I am starting out with polynomials. Polynomial functions are less valuable for geometry and more valuable for ideas like motion or consumption. For example, you can easily describe the motion of a car as a polynomial function of time. However, the rich curves of the curves of the car require something more flexible. In fact, Pierre Bezier invented Bezier curves while working for an automobile designer. I'll discuss this more in Chapter 3, "Paremetric Equations and Bezier Curves."

In the meantime, polynomial curves provide an easy framework in which to discuss some of the properties of curves.

What Is a Polynomial?

I have defined a curve as the graph of a function, so I should begin by defining a polynomial function.

At this point, even my chance of receiving Christmas cards from the mathematicians is pretty low. To put it another way, this means it takes the following form:

$$f(x) = C_0 x^N + C_1 x^{N-1} + C_1 x^{N-2} + \ldots + C_0 x^0$$

Equation 1.1   *The form of a polynomial function with a single variable.*

> **Definition**
>
> An nth degree polynomial function is defined as a series of n powers of one or more variables multiplied by constant coefficients.

This shows that the degree of the polynomial is the value of the highest exponent. Remember, some of the coefficients can be zero; this does not affect the degree. Therefore, the two following equations are both fourth-degree polynomials.

$f(x) = 5x^4 + 4x^3 + 3x^2 + 2x + 1$
$f(x) = 5x^4 + 2x + 1$

Equation 1.2   *Two equations of the same degree but different numbers of terms.*

According to my definitions, a polynomial curve is a graph of a polynomial function. The remainder of the chapters will focus on the properties of curves of different degrees. The simplest polynomial function is a first-degree polynomial known to its friends as a line.

Lines and Slopes

Although many people don't think of it this way, a line is a first-degree polynomial curve because the highest power is one. The two forms of the following line equation are equivalent. The first one fits the form shown in Equation 1.1 and the second is the form introduced in early math classes.

$f(x) = C_0 x + C_1$
$y = mx + b$

Equation 1.3   *Two forms of the equation for a line.*

The first coefficient (m in the second form) is the slope of the line. It defines how steeply the line angles as the values of the variable increase or decrease. The second coefficient is an offset. It defines a constant offset value for the line. Without the offset, all lines would pass through the point (0, 0) regardless of the slope. Figure 1.1 shows how the coefficients affect the line.

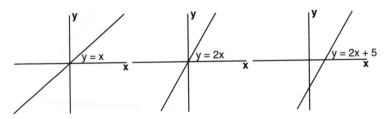

Figure 1.1   *Examples of lines.*

To put it a different way, the slope represents the ratio of the change in the result of the function to the change in the variable. This ratio is shown in Equation 1.4.

$$y = mx$$

$$m = \frac{y}{x}$$

Equation 1.4 *The slope as the ratio of y to x.*

In most cases, the slope of a line is much more interesting and important than the offset because it describes the direction of the line. The slope is the same for any point on the line, which makes it easier to visualize. For higher-degree polynomials, it isn't quite this simple. In the next section, I'll show you functions for which the slope is constantly changing. Throughout this book, you'll see ways in which the slope is very important.

Before I move to polynomials of a higher degree, I would like to remind you that mathematically, there is no difference between a polynomial with a degree of one and a polynomial with a higher degree. I have set them apart here so that you could begin to think about slopes in familiar terms, but you'll soon see that they all behave the same way.

Higher-Degree Polynomials

Consider, if you will, the selection of curves shown in Figure 1.2.

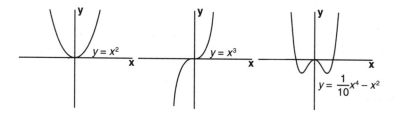

Figure 1.2 *Higher-degree polynomials.*

The last section talked quite a bit about slopes, but the curves in Figure 1.2 do not have a constant slope. In fact, the leftmost curve has a different slope at each and every point along the curve. At this point, life suddenly becomes more complicated. Figure 1.3 shows you why. Both pictures show a bullet moving along a path. In the left picture, the bullet is moving along a straight line. You can easily say that the direction of the bullet at any point along the path is the same as the slope of the line. In the right picture, the bullet follows a curved path. It is still true that the direction of the bullet matches the slope of the curve, but the direction changes.

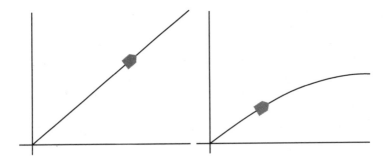

Figure 1.3 *Bullets along different paths.*

You can draw a curve without caring too much about the slope at any given point, but you can't correctly draw the bullet if you don't know how to find the slope at that point. This is where calculus comes in handy. If you aren't familiar with calculus, now might be a good time to jump ahead to Appendix A, "Derivative Calculus." I have included a short tutorial on differential calculus that will provide you with the basic tools you need to move forward.

You can find the slope at any point along the curve by finding the derivative of the curve at that point. For simple polynomials, this process is relatively easy because the functions are easy to differentiate. Once you know how to find the slope at any point, you can use derivatives to gain a better understanding of nearly any polynomial function.

As an example, let's say I tell you that the distance covered by a falling object is given by the following equation.

$$P(t) = \frac{1}{2}at^2$$

Equation 1.5 *Simple equation for the distance covered by a falling object.*

In fact, this equation is correct if you assume that the initial position and velocity are zero. From this, you can draw the graph in Figure 1.4.

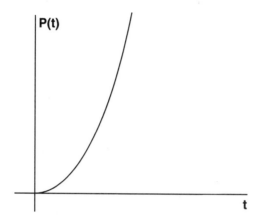

Figure 1.4 *The distance covered by a falling object over time.*

This graph shows that the object moved small distances at first, but large distances later. This would imply that the velocity grew over time. In fact, the velocity at any point in time is the slope of the position curve at that time. As outlined in Appendix A, you can find the slope using differential calculus. To find the velocity at time t, differentiate Equation 1.5 to get the following equation.

$$V(t) = \frac{dP(t)}{dt} = at$$

Equation 1.6 *The first derivative of Equation 1.5.*

Equation 1.6 describes how the position of an object changes as time changes. This is the speed of the object. Speed is how fast something changes with respect to time. It is also the first derivative of the distance.

If you graph Equation 1.6, you'll get the graph shown in Figure 1.5.

NOTE

Remember that speed and velocity are different. Speed is a simple scalar value. Velocity is a vector value. The distinction isn't terribly important in this context, but I don't want to lead you astray.

This is the graph of the values of the slope. In Figure 1.4, you could see that the slope was increasing. Figure 1.5 shows that the slope (and therefore the speed) is increasing linearly.

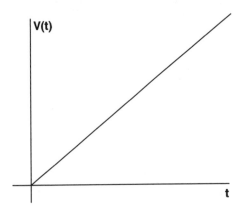

Figure 1.5   *The speed of a falling object over time.*

Now, go one step further and differentiate this. The derivative of speed is acceleration. Acceleration is the measure of how the speed changes over time. In this case, the derivative is a constant, as shown in Equation 1.7. Figure 1.6 shows the very simple resulting graph.

$$A(t) = \frac{dV(t)}{dt} = a$$

Equation 1.7   *The second derivative of Equation 1.5.*

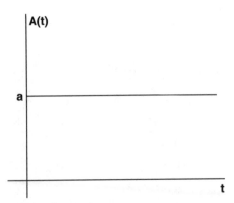

Figure 1.6   *The acceleration of a falling object over time.*

Figure 1.6 shows that the acceleration of the object was constant throughout time. This is true for falling objects. Gravity remains effectively constant unless you are talking about measuring very small changes and falling very long distances. So, you can see that the derivatives do accurately reflect what is actually happening.

Figure 1.7 condenses these three steps into three graphs. In this case, the equation for the distance is a polynomial of a higher degree. You can see that the acceleration is not constant. Instead, it increases linearly over time. These graphs could be showing the behavior of a car where the driver is slowly increasing pressure on the gas pedal over time.

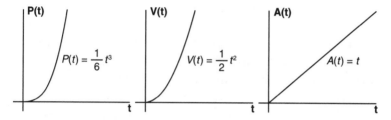

Figure 1.7   *The distance, speed, and acceleration of a moving object.*

In most cases, you will not need to derive these characteristics because you will know them already. The purpose of the preceding examples was to get you thinking about how curves work and the meaning behind the features of both the graphs and the equations. As the next section will show, you will have an easier time understanding and implementing the behavior of an object if you understand exactly how a curve is affecting that object.

Joining Curves and Continuity

Sometimes, you will want a curve to have different properties in different intervals like the one shown on the right side of Figure 1.8.

The left side shows an object moving at a constant speed. The problem is that it is a little too constant. The leftmost graph implies that the object instantaneously accelerated to the constant speed and then instantly decelerated at the end of the interval. The rightmost graph shows a more realistic example. The object accelerates smoothly to the constant speed and then later smoothly decelerates.

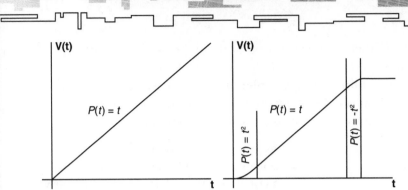

Figure 1.8 *Two graphs of distance over time.*

When you are joining multiple curves, one of the most important properties is continuity. You can talk about several orders of continuity and each level says something about the transition between the two curves. Curves with zero-order continuity are continuous graphs with no breaks. Curves with first-order continuity have continuous first derivatives (the graphs of their slopes are continuous). Curves with second-order continuity have continuous second derivatives, and so on. The orders of continuity are denoted as C^0, C^1, and so on.

In most cases, zero- and first-order continuities are extremely important because they have the most visible effect at the point where the curves are joined. Higher orders of continuity are generally less important because it isn't as noticeable when the higher derivatives of the curves do not match. Figure 1.9 shows two examples of curves joined with various forms of continuity. Notice that one order of continuity does not necessarily imply another.

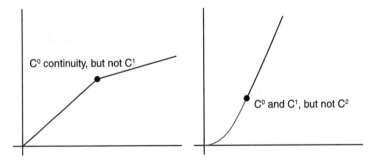

Figure 1.9 *Examples of curves with different orders of continuity.*

As you can see, C^0 continuity means that there is no gap between the two curves. The curves are joined, but there can be a kink at the join. An object moving along that path would experience an instantaneous change in velocity at the join. C^1 continuity means that the slopes of both curves match where they join, producing a smooth transition. An object moving along the path would experience a smoother change in velocity. Higher orders of continuity might be important in terms of velocity and acceleration, but their effects are typically less visually apparent.

This concept will become much more important when I get into Bezier curves and splines. In the meantime, experiment with joining some curves so that you can get a better sense of what needs to be done to establish different levels of continuity.

Introducing the Curve Application

Each chapter will include code that highlights the more important points of the chapter. I have chosen to make the applications very simple so that you can concentrate on the curve concepts rather than the details of rendering. That said, I will spend very little time talking about the specifics of rendering in order to save space. The code is written in DirectX, but it should be easy to re-create in OpenGL if you would rather do that. Remember that this code is written to highlight the curves and, therefore, it is not optimized at all.

The source code for this chapter can be found on the CD in the \Code\Chapter01 directory. Several of the files in that directory are for the basic framework and can be ignored if you would like (the framework is described in detail in *Real-Time Rendering Tricks and Techniques in DirectX*, Premier Press, ISBN 1-931841-27-6). Each application includes a base class that handles drawing the basic environment. It sets up the drawing canvas by drawing a grid of lines and a set of axes. It is important to note that the units for drawing the curve are in pixels. This will make things easier in later chapters, but for now it can be a hindrance because some polynomial functions will produce results that quickly move outside the bounds of the application window. To see what I mean, take a look at CurveApplication.cpp. This is the file that contains all of the chapter-specific code.

The code in CurveApplication.cpp is very simple. It is meant to introduce you to the application framework with the minimum of distractions and to illustrate the first derivative of polynomial functions. Figure 1.10 shows a screenshot of the application.

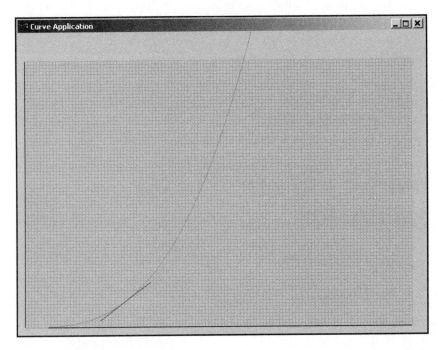

Figure 1.10 *A screenshot showing a sample curve and the slope at a given point.*

This first application draws a curve and also shows the slope at every point along the curve. You can set the function by redefining this macro at the top of the file.

```
#define FUNCTION_X(x) (0.00001f * (float)x * (float)x * (float)x)
```

In this case, the y values along the graph are equal to x cubed. I have multiplied it by a very small constant to keep the graph more reasonable. Try removing this constant. You'll see that the curve becomes so steep that it's not even worth looking at.

In this sample, you must specify the first derivative yourself. Do this by setting the second macro.

```
#define DERIVATIVE_X(x) (0.00003f * (float)x * (float)x)
```

Remember that you must include the scaling constant in the derivative as well. Feel free to experiment with different polynomial functions, but remember to include a scaling factor in all of your calculations.

Once the functions have been set, the application creates the vertices for the actual curve using the following code. The resolution of the curve defines how many points are created. A larger number for the resolution creates more spacing between the points, forming a lower resolution curve.

```
int Index = 0;
for (int x = 0; x <= 600; x += CURVE_RESOLUTION)
{
        pVertices[Index].x      = (float)x;
        pVertices[Index].y      = FUNCTION_X((float)x);
        pVertices[Index].z      = 1.0f;
        pVertices[Index].color = 0xFFFF0000;

        Index ++;
}
```

Figure 1.11 shows a lower resolution version of the same curve.

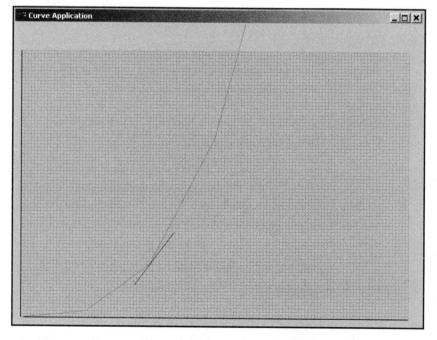

Figure 1.11   *A lower resolution version of the curve in Figure 1.10.*

The application uses these vertices to draw the curve every frame. In addition, the application also draws an animated slope line at the different points along the curve. It does this by setting the positions of two points using the following code. The current x value is based on the current system time. The modulo operator keeps the x position within the valid x range, but the result may still appear offscreen.

```
float CurrentX = (float)((GetTickCount() / 10) % 600);
```

The rest of the code includes a fair amount of trigonometry, which leads very well into the next chapter. This code uses arctangent to find the angle of the slope and then uses the angle value to figure out x and y positions with the help of the current position on the curve and the length of the slope line. Once these positions are computed, the application will draw the slope line.

```
float CurrentSlope = DERIVATIVE_X(CurrentX);
float CurrentAngle = atan(CurrentSlope);

pVertices[0].x = CurrentX + SLOPE_WIDTH * cos(CurrentAngle);
pVertices[0].y = FUNCTION_X(CurrentX) + SLOPE_WIDTH *
sin(CurrentAngle);
pVertices[0].z     = 1.0f;
pVertices[0].color = 0xFF0000FF;

pVertices[1].x = CurrentX - SLOPE_WIDTH * cos(CurrentAngle);
pVertices[1].y = FUNCTION_X(CurrentX) - SLOPE_WIDTH *
sin(CurrentAngle);
pVertices[1].z     = 1.0f;
pVertices[1].color = 0xFF0000FF;
```

Obviously, I have breezed past much of the code in this first application. The code will be very simple if you've worked with DirectX before. If not, take some time to experiment with the code before moving on. The rest of the chapters are based on the same basic ideas and framework.

In Conclusion...

I am moving fairly quickly because I suspect that this is review for most of the readers. If this is not the case, spend some time working with

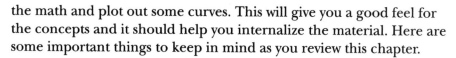
the math and plot out some curves. This will give you a good feel for the concepts and it should help you internalize the material. Here are some important things to keep in mind as you review this chapter.

- Most of my mathematical definitions are far from rigorous. There are entire books written on some of the ideas I cover in one sentence. Most of the proofs in those books are not necessary for the general practitioner. If you enjoy the material and want to know more, there are some very good books available. A few of them are described in Appendix C.

- Lines are first-degree polynomial functions. The slope of the line defines the direction and the slope is the same for all points along the line.

- Higher-degree polynomials require differentiation to determine the slope at any point along the curve. The derivative of a function is used to compute the slope for any value of the input variable.

- Continuity between two adjoining curves can be on many levels. Zero-order continuity means that the two curves are actually joined on the graph. Higher orders of continuity apply if higher derivatives of the functions are also continuous.

- The curve applications all share a common framework. The positions of the points on the curves are given in pixels, so you may need to scale accordingly when drawing higher-degree polynomials. This will become less of a burden in later chapters.

- So far, the concepts are fairly simple and atomic. Spend time with the concepts and read Appendix A if there are things you don't understand.

CHAPTER 2

TRIGONOMETRIC FUNCTIONS

T rigonometric functions and their curves are not used very often in this book, but they are still interesting because they provide useful ways of dealing with angles and because they are periodic (they have a repeating pattern). This chapter will provide a short introduction to trigonometry and introduce the following concepts.

- Definitions of sine, cosine, and tangent
- Definitions of the properties of a wave
- Some simple uses of trigonometric functions
- Taylor series approximations of trigonometric functions
- Aliasing

Defining Sine, Cosine, and Tangent

Trigonometry is the branch of mathematics that helps us understand angular relationships between the sides of triangles. Trigonometric functions are tools you can use to relate angles to distances and vice versa. Geometrically, these functions are based on the properties of a right triangle. In this chapter, I will concentrate on the three basic trigonometric functions: sine, cosine, and tangent. There are more, but these first three are the most useful for basic tasks. These functions are easy to understand if you begin by looking at a series of right triangles inscribed in a circle, as shown in Figure 2.1.

NOTE

Remember that all trigonometric functions take parameters measured in radians. If you are measuring angles in degrees, you may need to convert your units before passing them to the trigonometric functions. Remember that 360 degrees equals 2pi radians. Having said that, I will use degrees for many of my explanations simply because most people seem to think in degrees.

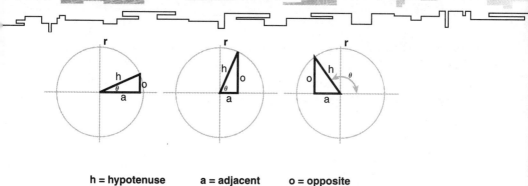

h = hypotenuse   a = adjacent   o = opposite

Figure 2.1   *Triangles inscribed in a circle.*

Each of the circles has a radius of r. Angles about the center of the circle are not measured in degrees. Instead, a full circle is 2pi radians.

As you can see, the lengths of the sides of each triangle change as the angles change. The three trigonometric functions are based on these changes. As Figure 2.1 shows, each side of the triangle can be defined relative to the angle. The sides are the hypotenuse, the adjacent side, and the opposite side. Sine, cosine, and tangent are defined as ratios of the lengths of those sides for any angle, as shown in the following equations.

$$\sin(\theta) = \frac{o}{h}$$

$$\cos(\theta) = \frac{a}{h}$$

$$\tan(\theta) = \frac{o}{a} = \frac{\sin(\theta)}{\cos(\theta)}$$

Equation 2.1   *Sine, cosine, and tangent.*

Note that on a unit circle (with a radius of 1.0), the ratios for sine and cosine are equal to the lengths of the opposite and adjacent sides respectively. All of the rest of the graphs in this chapter assume a unit circle. Tangent is a little different. It defines the ratio of the opposite and adjacent side. This is equivalent to the "rise over run" definition of the slope of a line. Therefore, tangent is the slope of the hypotenuse. A line that is tangent to a curve at a given point has the same slope as the slope of the curve at that point.

If you sketch out a few triangles like those shown in Figure 2.1, you'll see that the opposite and adjacent sides lengthen and shorten as the angle grows. Equation 2.1 shows that the lengths can be described by sine and cosine. Therefore, you can see exactly how the lengths change by graphing sine and cosine as shown in Figure 2.2. Note that the x-axis is now the angle theta, given in radians.

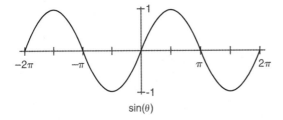

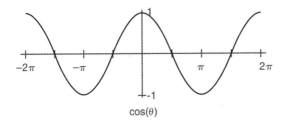

Figure 2.2 *Graphs of sine and cosine.*

The graphs are both the same shape, but they are offset by 90 degrees (pi/2 radians). This should come as no surprise. Sine basically gives you a vertical measurement. Cosine gives you a horizontal measurement. You can turn one into the other if you rotate the circle by pi/2 radians. I will address this later when I talk about phase.

Tangent is different. If you think of tangent as the slope of the hypotenuse, you can see that the slope changes from zero to infinity over the first 90 degrees. It then switches to negative infinity and back to zero over the second 90 degrees. Figure 2.3 shows a graph of the tangent function.

Figures 2.2 and 2.3 demonstrate the fact that these functions are periodic. This means that they repeat a specific pattern over specific time intervals (periods). Figure 2.4 shows one cycle of a sine wave. Its period is 2pi radians.

Sine, cosine, and tangent are useful functions for dealing with angles, but the sine wave pattern is useful simply by virtue of its shape and

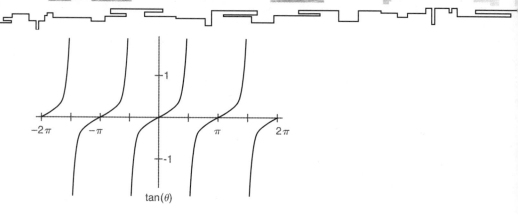

Figure 2.3 *Graph of tangent.*

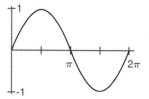

Figure 2.4 *One cycle of a sine wave.*

periodicity. Sine in particular is nice because each cycle of the wave oscillates between −1 and 1. In the next section, I will define the properties of a wave and discuss how they can be useful.

Properties of Waves

So far, I've talked generally about sine waves, but I haven't really shown an equation for them. The following shows an equation for a sine wave including all the properties that shape the wave. Figure 2.5 shows a plot of the wave, labeling those properties.

$$y = Amplitude * sin\left(\frac{1}{wavelength}\theta + phase\right)$$

Equation 2.2 *Sine wave equation.*

The sine function gives the overall shape, as shown in Figure 2.2. The amplitude parameter defines the maximum and minimum values for the values on the plot. If you refer back to Figure 2.1, the amplitude is equal to the radius of the circle.

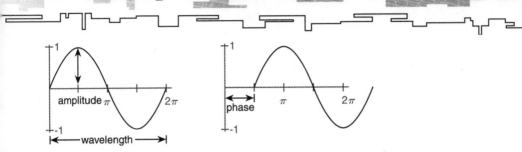

Figure 2.5 *Properties of waves.*

The wavelength is the length of one cycle of the wave. If you refer back to Figure 2.2, the wavelength of the basic sine function is obviously 2pi (360 degrees). After that, the wave repeats itself. The inverse of the wavelength is the frequency, or how many times the wave repeats itself in a certain interval. A shorter wavelength equals a higher frequency because more waves can fit in a given interval. In Equation 2.2, the frequency scales the angle value. If you plot this, you will see that this scaling factor causes more or less waves to be drawn in the same interval.

Finally, the phase is an offset. It shifts the wave along the x-axis by offsetting the angle parameter. As I pointed out before, the cosine wave is just an offset version of a sine wave. The following equation describes cosine as a function of sine.

$$\cos(\theta) = \sin\left(\theta + \frac{\pi}{2}\right)$$

Equation 2.3 *Cosine as a function of sine.*

Once you understand these properties, you'll be able to use sine waves in many different ways. In the next section, I will talk about a few of them, but I encourage you to experiment and become familiar with these concepts.

Some Simple Uses for Trigonometric Functions

The code for Chapter 1, "Polynomial Curves," featured some trigonometry that I promised I would explain in this chapter. The code illustrated the derivative of a curve by moving a straight line along the curve and tangent to the curve. Figure 2.6 is a screenshot from Chapter 1, only this time I have added lines to construct a right triangle like the one shown in Figure 2.1.

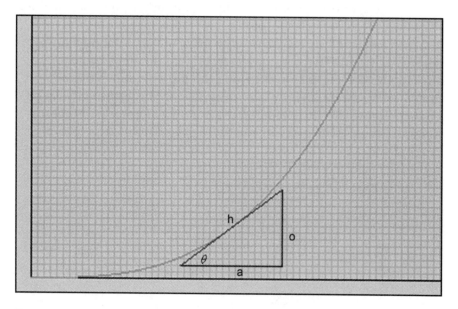

Figure 2.6   *Adding a triangle to the screenshot from Chapter 1.*

If you combine the derivative information from the last chapter with the trigonometric information from this chapter, you will get the following equation.

$$\tan(\theta) = \frac{o}{a} = \frac{dy}{dx}$$

Equation 2.4   *Equating slope and tangent.*

From that, you can get the angle of the line by using arctangent as shown in the next equation.

$$\theta = \arctan\left(\frac{dy}{dx}\right)$$

Equation 2.5   *Finding the angle with arctangent.*

NOTE

The inverse of each trigonometric function begins with "arc". These functions are arcsine, arccosine, and arctangent. The results of these functions are given in radians.

The angle itself isn't the end goal; you really want to find another point on the slope that defines that angle. Equation 2.5 gives you a value that you can feed back into the sine and cosine functions. These functions will give you the x and y values for another point on the line. Remember, the results of sine and cosine have a maximum value of 1.0, so you can scale the result by some value to make the line longer or shorter. Figure 2.7 shows graphically how all the steps come together to give you another point along the line that shows the slope. Once you have two points, you can draw a line. This technique will be used throughout the curve chapters to draw the slope at points along different curves.

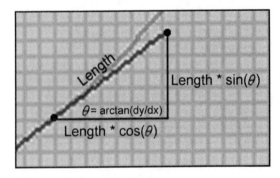

Figure 2.7 *Putting the pieces together.*

The preceding example shows one of the many uses for these functions as they relate to angles. Sine waves can be extremely useful for many applications. Imagine writing a very simple shooting gallery game where a target moves back and forth on the screen. That motion could be driven by a sine function. You could alter the limits of motion by changing the amplitude. You could also change the speed of the target by changing the frequency.

The code for this chapter can be found in the \Code\Chapter02 directory on the CD. It is nearly identical to the code from Chapter 1, but I have added two functions that illustrate interesting wave applications. Use this code as a starting point for your own experimentation.

The first application shows a very simple way to generate interesting behaviors. If you are writing a hockey game, you don't want the players to always skate in straight lines. Instead, you might compute the basic path of a player and then use a sine wave to oscillate along that path.

The function for this is shown next and a screenshot is shown in Figure 2.8.

```
#define FUNCTION_THETA(x) (x + 50.0f * sin(0.1f * (float)x))
#define DERIVATIVE_THETA(x) (1 + 5.0f * cos(0.1f * (float)x))
```

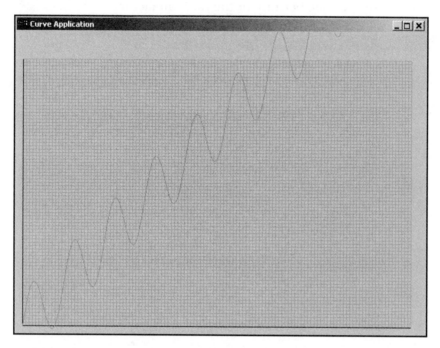

Figure 2.8   *Oscillating along a line.*

You could generate different behaviors for each player on the team by tweaking the parameters of the wave equation. You could also use small random changes to make the motion less predictable. Obviously, you can do much more to determine and adjust the behaviors of the players, but this is one starting point.

A different application of the same technique could be used to generate fake stock market data. You could use a high-amplitude, low-frequency wave to generate the general trend of the stock. You could then use smaller high-frequency waves to generate the daily trading activity. The following code shows a simple example of that.

```
#define GENERAL_TREND(x)  (350.0f * sin(0.0035f * (float)x))
#define RANDOM            (float)rand() / (float)RAND_MAX
```

```
#define DAILY (x) (40.0f * RANDOM * sin(0.035f * (float)x + 10.0f *
RANDOM))
#define FUNCTION_THETA(x) GENERAL_TREND(x) + DAILY (x)
```

Figure 2.9 shows a screenshot of this. The derivative functionality does
not work for this sample because of the random factors.

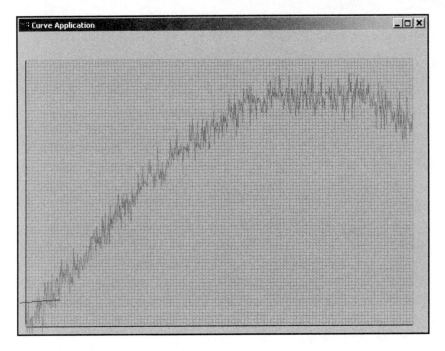

Figure 2.9   *Simple stock data simulation.*

Again, you would probably want to do more to model real stock fluc-
tuations, but this type of approach shows you how a periodic function
could be used to very quickly generate something passable.

Whenever you are modeling something periodic, consider using a sine
wave as your basic primitive. The fact that it is periodic and bounded
by –1 and 1 make it convenient for many tasks. There are occasions
where using standard API functions like sin() may be impractical, or in
the case of DirectX vertex shaders, nonexistent. That's when you
might want to compute sine yourself.

Computing Trigonometric Functions with Taylor Series Approximations

Although it is outside the scope of this book to explain why, it is important to note that you can approximate trigonometric functions using an approximation of an infinite polynomial known as the Taylor series. The Taylor series expansions for sine and cosine are shown next.

$$\sin(x) = x - \frac{x^3}{3!} + \frac{x^5}{5!} - \frac{x^7}{7!}$$

$$\cos(x) = 1 - \frac{x^2}{2!} + \frac{x^4}{4!} - \frac{x^6}{6!}$$

Equation 2.6 *Taylor series expansions.*

These equations have an infinite number of terms, but you don't normally have an infinite amount of time. Therefore, you want to approximate the value by taking a set number of terms. You can usually get by with a small number of terms; you just need to understand how they converge. Figure 2.10 shows several graphs of sine using different numbers of terms in the Taylor series. As you can see, four terms are sufficient to get decent results for values in the interval of –pi to pi.

Obviously, four terms are not sufficient for any value outside the –pi to pi interval, but remember that these functions are periodic. Therefore, any value of theta can be mapped into that interval using the following equation.

$$\theta_{mapped} = 2\pi((\theta + \pi)\bmod(2\pi)) - \pi$$

Equation 2.7 *Mapping angle values back to a limited range.*

The basic idea is that it shifts theta by pi and finds the modulo of the result and 2pi. It then multiplies that by 2pi and subtracts pi. The result is the equivalent value in the range of –pi to pi. Equations 2.6 and 2.7 can be used to compute results for any angle value with relatively few terms. When you do this yourself, experiment with the number of terms until you get the accuracy you need.

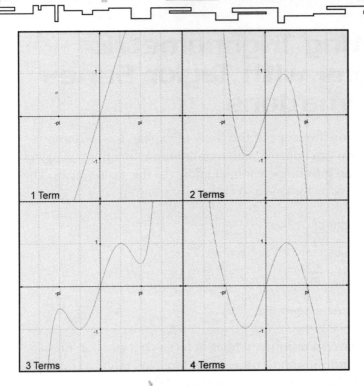

Figure 2.10   *Taylor series approximations.*

Aliasing

Aliasing is a signal processing phenomenon that could come up if you work with sine waves. The best way to introduce this is by example. Imagine I gave you a sine wave with a frequency of one cycle per second (1Hz) and I asked you to tell me the frequency of that wave. You could give me accurate results if you sampled the wave at frequencies of 2Hz or greater. This is shown in Figure 2.11.

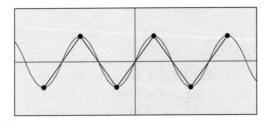

Figure 2.11   *Sampling a sine wave at twice the frequency.*

Now, imagine I gave you a 4Hz wave, but I limited your sampling rate to 2Hz. As Figure 2.12 shows, you'd mistakenly conclude that this new wave was a 2Hz signal.

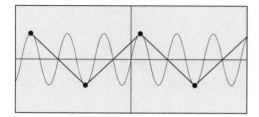

Figure 2.12   *Aliasing while sampling at a low rate.*

Aliasing happens when your sampling frequency is less than twice the signal frequency. In signal processing, this is called the Nyquist frequency.

You may think that this would not apply to game development, but it could. Think back to the hockey player example. Using a sinusoidal function, the position of the player might be computed every frame. Therefore, the frame rate is your sampling frequency into that function. If the frame rate is too low, the results may be confusing. For instance, imagine you pick a frequency that looks good but was actually aliased. Later, you run your hockey game on a faster computer and suddenly the player is skating wildly back and forth. The code could be totally correct, but aliasing could have caused you to pick a bad frequency.

In Conclusion...

If the material in this chapter was not review for you, please experiment with some of the functions. Use the circle drawings to plot out several curves. Also, read Appendix A to get an explanation of how to compute the derivative of trigonometric functions. These functions are not used too often in the rest of the chapters, but I thought there were several concepts that were worth talking about. Trigonometry is extremely useful for dealing with angles and you will work with angles frequently in game development. Before moving on to the new material, let me enumerate some of the more important points from this chapter.

- Trigonometry is used to describe the relationship between the angle of a line and the x and y distances it covers.

- Sine, cosine, and tangent are the three most frequently used functions. They describe the ratios of the sides of triangles as a function of an angle.
- All three functions are periodic.
- The exact shape of a wave is determined by its amplitude, wavelength, and phase.
- The frequency of a wave is the inverse of its wavelength.
- Trigonometric functions can be approximated with Taylor series representations.

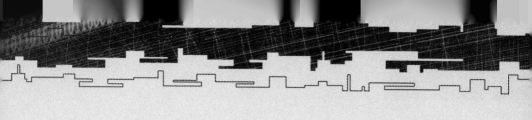

PART TWO

FOCUS ON
CURVES

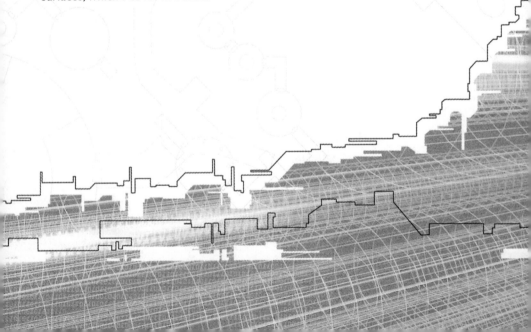

This is where the real material on curves actually begins. Curves can be very useful for many applications. They can be used to define paths for objects in a game world; they can be used as functions that describe the speed, color, or other attributes of the objects; and, of course, they can be used to draw curves on the screen. These curves could be used to define and draw anything from fonts to strands of hair and fur. In the samples, I have chosen to draw the curves as basic shapes rather than try to implement a specific example of fur or some other "real-world" application. There are a couple of reasons for this. First, I have a limited amount of space and I want to make sure I cover the important topics. Second, I don't want someone to get the impression that any one of these concepts is directly tied to some specific application. By not giving you too many specific examples, I hope that you will be more open to finding your own interesting applications. Therefore, the sample code doesn't tell you how to draw grass; it simply shows you how to draw curves.

I begin by walking you through Bezier curves, which are straightforward but limited examples of parametric curves. From there, I will explain B-splines, which are a more general and flexible approach to drawing curves. From there, I will talk about NURBS (NonUniform Rational B-Splines), which are an even more flexible approach.

Each chapter concentrates on the mechanics of the different types of curves and renders those curves in the most straightforward way possible. This section of the book will be wrapped up in Chapter 6 where I will explain how to subdivide curves to produce more efficient rendering.

These curves are useful on their own, and they also serve as the foundation for surfaces, which I cover in Part 3.

CHAPTER 3

PARAMETRIC EQUATIONS AND BEZIER CURVES

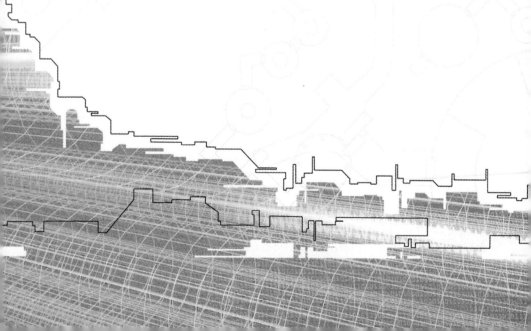

In Chapter 1, "Polynomial Curves," I talked about polynomial functions and the curves you can draw with them. It might have been clear from that discussion that polynomial functions are not very flexible for drawing curves of arbitrary shapes. In this chapter, I will present an alternative representation for curves (parametric equations) that will serve as a foundation for the remaining chapters. I will show you how parametric equations are used to draw Bezier curves. Along the way, I will cover the following concepts.

- What is a parametric equation?
- Bezier curves defined with parametric equations
- Bezier curve basis functions and their derivatives
- Limitations of Bezier curves
- Joining Bezier curves
- Drawing Bezier curves

What Is a Parametric Equation?

In Chapter 1, I started with a line as the simplest example of a polynomial curve and I gave the equation for a line in terms of its slope and an offset. This is a mathematically correct form, and the form you usually learn first in school, but it is also fairly limited in how it can be used in practical applications because it doesn't explicitly handle some of the issues that come up when you are writing code.

For example, a math teacher will tell you that a vertical line has a slope that is undefined because of the "rise over run" definition of the slope. This is mathematically true, but it is inconvenient to think of your rocket ship as traveling along a path that is "undefined". Also, the simple equation for a line is not explicitly bounded by two endpoints, yet nearly all lines you draw will be based on explicit endpoints. For these and other reasons, it would be advantageous to have an alternate representation for a line.

This is where parametric equations come in handy. Imagine the following scenario. I tell you to walk from point A to point B beginning at time t=0 and ending at time t=1. Your position, P, at any given time throughout your journey will be a function of A, B, and t, as shown in Figure 3.1.

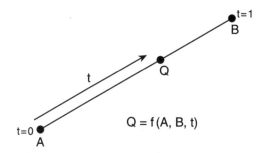

Figure 3.1 *Describing a path along a line.*

If you wanted to use the line equation from Chapter 1, you could use the two points to find the slope and the offset. You could then have an equation that defined y in terms of x. If you wanted to find point Q, you'd have to choose a value for the x component of point Q and then compute the y component. If the slope is undefined, you would have to account for that as a special case. Instead, Figure 3.1 shows that you can formulate a line equation based on a parameter, t. The result is a parametric form of the line equation as shown next.

$$P(t) = Bt + A(1-t)$$

Equation 3.1 *The parametric equation for a line.*

My example implies that the variable t stands for time. In some cases this might be true, but it is more generally true to think of t as the normalized distance along the length of the path formed by the two endpoints. So, you can find the location of any point along the line with Equation 3.1. This can be convenient because you can think in terms of the line itself. For instance, the position of the midpoint becomes trivial. Simply use 0.5 for the value of t.

It should also be clear that the parametric form obviates the need to handle vertical lines with special code. Equation 3.1 works equally well for lines of any orientation. Also, it works well for lines in any number of dimensions. Equation 3.1 does not explicitly refer to x and y values because the same form is useful for 2D lines, 3D lines, or even higher. However, just to be clear, Equation 3.2 shows a more detailed view of how you compute the actual points.

$$P_x(t) = B_x t + A_x(1-t)$$
$$P_y(t) = B_y t + A_y(1-t)$$
$$P_z(t) = B_z t + A_z(1-t)$$

Equation 3.2 *Computing the output of the parametric equation.*

So, the parametric form allows you to think of curves as functions of a set of control points and a parameter that corresponds to a distance along the length of the curve. As you will see in this chapter and most of the others, this form is much more flexible and powerful than the form you learned in Chapter 1 or your math classes. Having said that, the concepts in Chapter 1 are still valuable because parametric functions are still polynomials. The only difference is that they are now polynomial functions of t instead of x. All the rules in Chapter 1 and Appendix A hold true for parametric equations. In fact, before I move on to actual curves, I should talk a little bit about how to find the derivative of a parametric equation.

Derivatives of Parametric Equations

In Chapter 1 and Appendix A, I talked about how the slope corresponded to a derivative and how that can be thought of as "the change in y with respect to x". Now I have given you parametric equations as functions of t, so it might appear that you need something different. It's actually quite easy. Both x and y change with respect to the common parameter t. You can compute the derivative, as shown in Equation 3.3.

$$\frac{dy}{dx} = \frac{\frac{dy}{dt}}{\frac{dx}{dt}}$$

Equation 3.3 *The derivative of a parametric equation.*

In most of the remaining chapters, the parametric equations will be polynomial functions of t, so derivatives can easily be computed as described in Appendix A. For clarity, Equation 3.4 shows how this is done for a simple line. You will see more interesting examples when I begin to talk about slopes on a Bezier curve.

$$\frac{dy}{dx} = \frac{\dfrac{d(B_y t + A_y - A_y t)}{dt}}{\dfrac{d(B_x t + A_x - A_x t)}{dt}} = \frac{B_y - A_y}{B_x - A_x} = \frac{rise}{run}$$

Equation 3.4 *The derivative of a line using a parametric equation.*

Bezier Curves Defined in Parametric Terms

Prior to CAD/CAM tools and high-precision machining, engineers and draftsmen drew curves in very imprecise ways. Typically, they would mark a few points along the curve and then use a French curve or something similar to draw a best-fit curve through the points. This approach became unacceptable with the introduction of computer-aided manufacturing because suddenly, automated machines could make very precise parts, but there was no way to describe these precise parts. Pierre Bezier was confronted with this problem while working for Renault in the 1960s. He invented Bezier curves as a way of precisely describing every point along a given curve. Computer-driven manufacturing machines could now be used to precisely and reliably produce the curve. Like most great inventions, other inventors were doing similar work simultaneously, but Bezier's name is the one that has been attached to this particular invention.

> **NOTE**
>
> In Chapter 4, "B-Splines," you will learn that Bezier curves can be thought of as a specific case of B-splines. In this chapter, I will explain them in strictly parametric terms in order to set the stage for the more general formulation of B-splines.

Some of the mathematical concepts that led up to the formulation of Bezier curves are beyond the scope of this book and not terribly

important for the practical user, so I will describe the formulation in basic
geometric terms. I have talked about simple parametric equations for
lines. Now, I will extend those concepts to curves. To go beyond a simple
linear curve, you need at least three points. These three points are called
control points and you can connect them to form a *control polygon*. Figure 3.2
shows a quadratic curve derived from three control points.

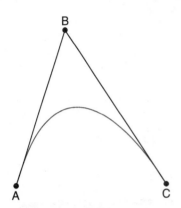

Figure 3.2 *Three control points
and the resulting quadratic curve.*

Before I talk about how to create this curve with parametric equations,
consider a very simple geometric approach. The curve in Figure 3.2
can be created using a basic subdivision technique. For each line
segment, create a point at the midpoint and join the resulting points.
Repeat this until the line segments are very short and you generate a
smooth curve. Figure 3.3 shows several steps of this technique.

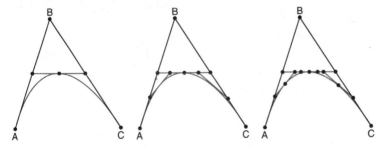

Figure 3.3 *Creating the quadratic curve with subdivision.*

If your only task was drawing this one curve, the geometric method
would be all you need. In a real situation, you'd quickly find that this

technique is fairly limited. If any of the points changed, you'd have to repeat all of the subdivision steps to produce even a single point. Clearly, you would like a way to describe any point along the curve as a function of the control points. This would allow you to compute points as a function of the control points without subdividing the entire curve. This sounds like a job for a parametric function.

Figure 3.4 shows the same set of control points as Figure 3.2, only now I am defining points along the two line segments using the parametric line equation shown in Equation 3.1.

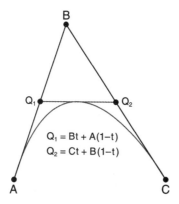

Figure 3.4 *Describing points on the two line segments.*

Now, connect Q1 and Q2. Figure 3.5 shows how the point Q3 can be described with a parametric equation involving Q1 and Q2.

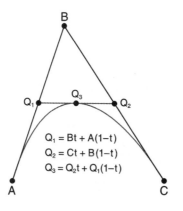

Figure 3.5 *Connecting the points with another parametric line.*

So, for any value of t, you can find a point on each line segment, connect them, and find a point on the new line segment. This point is Q3 from Figure 3.5. The location of Q3 is a function of t and the points Q1 and Q2, which are given by functions of A, B, C, and t. Therefore, you can collapse these individual parametric equations to yield the location of Q3 as a function of the control points and t as shown in the following set of equations (see Equation 3.5).

$$Q_1 = Bt + A(1-t)$$
$$Q_2 = Ct + B(1-t)$$
$$Q_3 = Q_2 t + Q_1(1-t)$$
$$Q_3 = Ct^2 + Bt(1-t) + Bt(1-t) + A(1-t)^2$$
$$Q_3 = A(1-t)^2 + 2Bt(1-t) + Ct^2$$

Equation 3.5   *Q3 as a parametric function of the control points.*

The final form of Equation 3.5 will yield the same quadratic curve shown in Figures 3.2 and 3.3. This is in fact the equation for a quadratic Bezier curve. You can restate this equation as the sum of a set of *basis functions* multiplied by the corresponding control point. Equation 3.6 shows how these equations are normally stated.

$$P(t) = \sum_{i=0}^{N} B_i(t)P_i$$

Equation 3.6   *Point on a Bezier curve expressed in terms of basis functions.*

These basis functions are known as Bernstein polynomials. They determine how much each control point influences the curve for any value of t. The three basis functions shown in Equation 3.6 correspond to a set of three control points, but Bezier curves can have any number of control points. The Bernstein polynomials for a given number of control points can be determined with the following equation.

$$B_i(t) = \frac{N! \, t^i (1-t)^{N-i}}{i!(N-i)!}$$

$$0^0 = 1$$
$$0! = 1$$

Equation 3.7 *The general equation for Bernstein polynomials.*

The disadvantage of using more control points is that the amount of computation for each point on the curve grows as the number of control points increases. Therefore, most people limit the number of points to either three or four. For the remainder of this chapter, I will be talking about four control points, which yield a cubic Bezier curve. The basis functions for cubic curves can be derived from Equation 3.7, but they are explicitly shown in Equation 3.8 for clarity.

$$B_0(t) = (1-t)^3$$
$$B_1(t) = 3t(1-t)^2$$
$$B_2(t) = 3t^2(1-t)$$
$$B_3(t) = t^3$$

Equation 3.8 *Four basis functions for a cubic Bezier curve.*

In this and other chapters, it is sometimes useful to be able to visualize the basis functions. Figure 3.6 shows graphs of the four basis functions as functions of t. The interval for t is [0, 1] and the range of the basis functions is also [0, 1].

Figure 3.6 reveals several characteristics of the basis functions and of Bezier curves in general. First of all, the sum of all the basis functions at any value of t is equal to 1. Also, each basis function affects every point along the curve except at the endpoints, where only the first and last control points affect the first and last points. Therefore, the endpoints of the control polygon are also the endpoints of the curve itself.

Figure 3.6 also reveals some serious limitations of Bezier curves. Each control point affects every point along the curve (except the extreme endpoints). This means many control points will require more computations when evaluating points on the curve. The result is that the

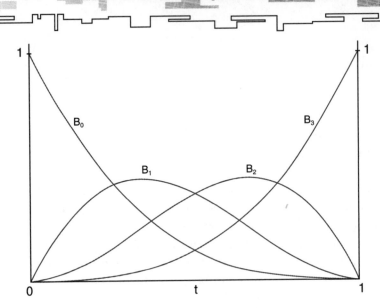

Figure 3.6 *Graphs of the four basis functions.*

number of control points determines the degree of the curve. The degree of the curve is always one less than the number of control points. Also, any changes to any of the control points will change every point along the curve (except the endpoints) in some way. This means that you have no *local control*. This is a problem with Bezier curves (and third-world governments) and it severely limits the amount of flexibility you have when determining the final shape of the curve. For these reasons, people will typically form curves by stringing together several cubic curves instead of forming one curve with many control points. This is a great time to talk about how to do that.

Joining Bezier Curves

Joining multiple Bezier curves is very easy because the curve always begins and ends at the end control points. You can achieve C^0 continuity by using the same control point for both the end of one curve and the start of the next. Depending on your implementation, you may actually use two points that have the same location, but the bottom line is that collocated control points at the end of the curve ensure that the curve itself is C^0 continuous.

You can join two curves with C^1 continuity almost as easily. The slope at the endpoint of a Bezier curve is equal to the slope of the last line segment in the control polygon. Therefore, curves can maintain C^1 continuity if the last and first line segments are collinear. For the most part, these first two levels of continuity are all that you will need to worry about when you want to smoothly join two curves. Figure 3.7 shows examples of curves with different levels of continuity. The upper curves are joined, but there is a kink at the join. The lower curves are joined with matching slopes, producing a smooth transition.

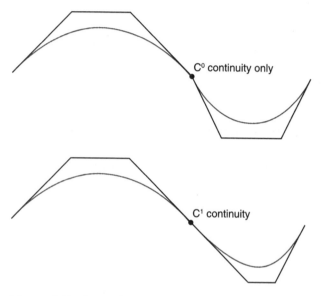

Figure 3.7 *Joining Bezier curves.*

Finding Derivatives of Bezier Curves

A discussion of higher levels of continuity necessarily leads to a discussion about how you find the derivatives of points on Bezier curves. Earlier in this chapter, Equation 3.3 demonstrated how you can find the 2D slope of a parametric equation by first finding the derivatives with respect to t. Bezier curves are no different other than the fact that their derivatives are more complicated than the linear form shown in Equation 3.4.

Equations 3.5 and 3.6 expressed the location of a point along a curve as a function of t and the set of control points. In the context of a derivative with respect to t, the control points are constants. Also, the equation for a Bezier curve is just the sum of these points multiplied by the results of their basis functions. Appendix A tells you that the derivative of a sum is the sum of the derivatives. If you put this all together, you will see that the equation for the derivative at any point on the curve is shown in Equation 3.9.

$$\frac{P(t)}{dt} = \sum_{i=0}^{N} \frac{dB_i(t)}{dt} P_i$$

Equation 3.9   *Equation for the derivative with respect to t.*

Now, you just need to find the derivatives of the basis functions. If you have had a calculus class, you know some more straightforward methods for solving for the derivatives for the basis functions shown in Equation 3.8. If not, you can expand the basis functions out to their polynomial form and find the derivative as explained in Appendix A. This method would yield the derivatives shown in Equation 3.10.

$$\frac{B_0(t)}{dt} = -3t^2 + 6t - 3$$

$$\frac{B_1(t)}{dt} = 9t^2 - 12t + 3$$

$$\frac{B_2(t)}{dt} = -9t^2 + 6t$$

$$\frac{B_3(t)}{dt} = 3t^2$$

Equation 3.10   *The derivatives of the basis functions.*

Between Equations 3.9 and 3.3, you have all the pieces you need to find dy/dx, or the 2D slope at any point on the Bezier curve.

Putting It All Together

The code for this chapter can be found on the CD in the \Chapter03 folder. BezierCurveApplication.cpp contains all of the new code related to the subject of Bezier curves. The code is very simple, but it demonstrates everything you need to know about drawing Bezier curves. However, you should remember that none of the code in this book is optimized for performance. The emphasis is more on clarity and ease of explanation. If you'd like, you can see a higher-performance sample in *Real-Time Rendering Tricks and Techniques in DirectX*. I feature one example where a Bezier surface is drawn with the help of vertex shaders. That book also pays more attention to performance considerations.

The code begins with a set of definitions. I have hard-coded the basis functions, their derivatives, and a simple animation function. Remember, this code assumes you are dealing with four control points.

```
//Basis functions
#define B0(t) ((1.0f - t) * (1.0f - t) * (1.0f - t))
#define B1(t) (3.0f * t * (1.0f - t) * (1.0f - t))
#define B2(t) (3.0f * t * t * (1.0f - t))
#define B3(t) (t * t * t)


//Derivatives of the basis functions
#define dB0(t) ((6.0f * t) - (3.0f * t * t) - 3.0f)
#define dB1(t) (3.0f - (12.0f * t) + (9.0f * t * t))
#define dB2(t) ((6.0f * t) - (9.0f * t * t))
#define dB3(t) (3.0f * t * t)


#define SLOPE_WIDTH 50.0f


#define ANIMATE(x) (x * sin((float)GetTickCount() / 1000.0f))
```

The application animates the control points and refills the vertex buffer every frame. The FillCurveBuffer function does the majority of the work.

```
BOOL CBezierCurveApplication::FillCurveBuffer()
{
        if (!m_pCurveVertices)
```

```
        return FALSE;
```

```
    GENERAL_VERTEX *pVertices;
```

The vertex buffer is set up to hold the four control vertices (used to draw the control polygon), two vertices used to draw the slope, and a set of vertices that make up the actual curve. This function locks the whole buffer and sets all of these vertices.

```
    if (FAILED(m_pCurveVertices->Lock(0,
                (6 + NUM_CURVE_VERTICES) * sizeof(GENERAL_VERTEX),
                (BYTE **)&pVertices, D3DLOCK_DISCARD)))
        return FALSE;
```

I begin by setting the control points. I have used a very simple animation function to provide some movement. You can change the function or change the values to see different curves. Note that all the values here are given as pixel coordinates.

```
    pVertices[0].x = 100.0f + ANIMATE(100.0f);
    pVertices[0].y = 100.0f + ANIMATE(100.0f);
    pVertices[1].x = 300.0f;
    pVertices[1].y = 200.0f + ANIMATE(200.0f);
    pVertices[2].x = 400.0f + ANIMATE(50.0f);
    pVertices[2].y = 200.0f;
    pVertices[3].x = 600.0f;
    pVertices[3].y = 100.0f + ANIMATE(-100.0f);

    pVertices[0].color = pVertices[1].color =
                         pVertices[2].color =
                         pVertices[3].color = 0xFF000000;

    pVertices[0].z = pVertices[1].z =
                     pVertices[2].z =
                     pVertices[3].z = 1.0f;
```

This code sets the position for every point along the curve. It is actually very simple once you have defined the basis functions. This just finds the x and y values based on the basis functions and the control points that were just animated. Note that I am offsetting the index of the vertex by 6 to account for the control vertices and slope vertices in the beginning of the buffer. In this case, the code assumes that there are at most, 100 points on the curve.

```
int Index = 0;
for (int i = 0; i <= 100; i += CURVE_RESOLUTION)
{
```

The value for t is found by dividing the value of i by 100. This yields a value of t between 0 and 1. This value is then used by the basis functions.

```
float t = (float)i / 100.0f;
```

```
pVertices[Index + 6].x     = (B0(t) * pVertices[0].x) +
                             (B1(t) * pVertices[1].x) +
                             (B2(t) * pVertices[2].x) +
                             (B3(t) * pVertices[3].x);
pVertices[Index + 6].y     = (B0(t) * pVertices[0].y) +
                             (B1(t) * pVertices[1].y) +
                             (B2(t) * pVertices[2].y) +
                             (B3(t) * pVertices[3].y);
pVertices[Index + 6].z     = 1.0f;
pVertices[Index + 6].color = 0xFFFF0000;

Index ++;
}
```

This function is used to animate the point of interest when drawing the slope of the curve. It basically finds the current tick count on the system, changes it to a value between 1 and 100, and divides that value by 100 to yield a final value for t between 0 and 1.

```
float Point = (float)((GetTickCount() / 100) % 100) / 100.0f;
```

The following code finds the current point of interest based on the value of t. This is basically the same code as shown above, only this time it is only applied to the current location of the slope line.

```
float PointX = (B0(Point) * pVertices[0].x) +
               (B1(Point) * pVertices[1].x) +
               (B2(Point) * pVertices[2].x) +
               (B3(Point) * pVertices[3].x);
float PointY = (B0(Point) * pVertices[0].y) +
               (B1(Point) * pVertices[1].y) +
               (B2(Point) * pVertices[2].y) +
               (B3(Point) * pVertices[3].y);
```

The following lines are used to find dx/dt and dy/dt.

```
float SlopeRun  = (dB0(Point) * pVertices[0].x) +
                  (dB1(Point) * pVertices[1].x) +
                  (dB2(Point) * pVertices[2].x) +
                  (dB3(Point) * pVertices[3].x);
float SlopeRise = (dB0(Point) * pVertices[0].y) +
                  (dB1(Point) * pVertices[1].y) +
                  (dB2(Point) * pVertices[2].y) +
                  (dB3(Point) * pVertices[3].y);
```

The slope can then be determined as shown in Equation 3.3. The remainder of the code sets the slope vertices as seen in the previous two chapters.

```
float Slope = SlopeRise / SlopeRun;
float Angle = atan(Slope);

pVertices[4].x = PointX + SLOPE_WIDTH * cos(Angle);
pVertices[4].y = PointY + SLOPE_WIDTH * sin(Angle);
pVertices[5].x = PointX - SLOPE_WIDTH * cos(Angle);
pVertices[5].y = PointY - SLOPE_WIDTH * sin(Angle);
pVertices[4].z = pVertices[5].z = 1.0f;
pVertices[4].color = pVertices[5].color = 0xFF0000FF;

m_pCurveVertices->Unlock();

return TRUE;
}
```

Finally, the curve is actually drawn with the Render function.

```
void CBezierCurveApplication::Render()
{
    CCurveApplication::Render();

    FillCurveBuffer();

    m_pD3DDevice->SetStreamSource(0, m_pCurveVertices,
                            sizeof(GENERAL_VERTEX));
```

These lines draw the slope line first, followed by the curve and the control polygon. I chose the drawing order to best show the relationship between all three pieces, but you can change the order or turn off specific parts if you'd like.

```
m_pD3DDevice->DrawPrimitive(D3DPT_LINESTRIP, 4, 1);
m_pD3DDevice->DrawPrimitive(D3DPT_LINESTRIP, 6,
NUM_CURVE_VERTICES - 1);
m_pD3DDevice->DrawPrimitive(D3DPT_LINESTRIP, 0, 3);
}
```

Figure 3.8 shows a screenshot of the resulting application. Notice the line that shows the slope. You will get a better view by actually running the animated application.

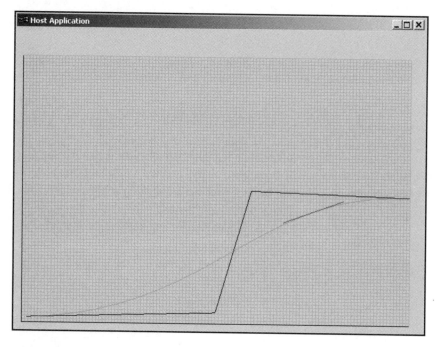

Figure 3.8   *A screenshot of the application.*

I have also included a function that draws the basis functions. This code was used to generate Figure 3.6. The function is a very bad example of performance coding because it generates a new vertex buffer each time it draws. It is included simply as a way to view the basis functions.

```
void CBezierCurveApplication::DrawBasisFunctions()
{
```

```
LPDIRECT3DVERTEXBUFFER8 pBasisVertices;
```

I create 400 vertices, 100 for each of the four basis functions.

```
if (FAILED(m_pD3DDevice->CreateVertexBuffer(
                    400 * sizeof(GENERAL_VERTEX),
                    D3DUSAGE_WRITEONLY |
                    D3DUSAGE_DYNAMIC,
                    D3DFVF_GENERALVERTEX,
                    D3DPOOL_DEFAULT, &pBasisVertices)))
        return;

GENERAL_VERTEX *pVertices;



if (FAILED(pBasisVertices->Lock(0, 400 * sizeof(GENERAL_VERTEX),
                            (BYTE **)&pVertices,
                            D3DLOCK_DISCARD)))
        return;
```

The following code sets the vertices for all four curves at one time. The code scales the values to fill the window by multiplying i by 6 and multiplying the results of the basis function by 400. See Figure 3.6 for the proper ranges for t and the basis functions.

```
for (long i = 0; i < 100; i++)
{
        float t = (float)i / 99.0f;

        pVertices[i].x            = i * 6;
        pVertices[i + 100].x      = i * 6;
        pVertices[i + 200].x      = i * 6;
        pVertices[i + 300].x      = i * 6;
        pVertices[i].y            = 400.0f * B0(t);
        pVertices[i + 100].y      = 400.0f * B1(t);
        pVertices[i + 200].y      = 400.0f * B2(t);
        pVertices[i + 300].y      = 400.0f * B3(t);
        pVertices[i].z = pVertices[i + 100].z =
                    pVertices[i + 200].z =
                    pVertices[i + 300].z = 1.0f;
```

```
            pVertices[i].color = pVertices[i + 100].color =
                                 pVertices[i + 200].color =
                                 pVertices[i + 300].color = 0xFFFF0000;
    }

    pBasisVertices->Unlock();
```

The curves are drawn by the following code.

```
    m_pD3DDevice->SetStreamSource(0, pBasisVertices,
                                  sizeof(GENERAL_VERTEX));
    m_pD3DDevice->DrawPrimitive(D3DPT_LINESTRIP, 0, 99);
    m_pD3DDevice->DrawPrimitive(D3DPT_LINESTRIP, 100, 99);
    m_pD3DDevice->DrawPrimitive(D3DPT_LINESTRIP, 200, 99);
    m_pD3DDevice->DrawPrimitive(D3DPT_LINESTRIP, 300, 99);

    pBasisVertices->Release();
}
```

Feel free to experiment with the positions of the control points to see the curves that they yield. Also, you may want to experiment with joining multiple curves. I will leave that up to you.

In Conclusion...

This chapter has set the stage for most of the curve concepts you'll see throughout the rest of this book. Bezier curves have their limitations, but they are a little bit easier to deal with than the more general B-splines. Before you move on to the next chapter, make sure you understand this chapter as much as possible. Here is a list of some of the things you should remember.

- Parametric equations are more flexible than the forms seen in earlier chapters, in part because they allow you to define a shape with control points rather than an abstract mathematical equation. They are the first example of parametric curve equations found in this and later chapters.

- Slopes of parametric curves can be computed by first finding the derivatives with respect to t.

- Bezier curves are defined in parametric terms as functions of a set of control points and basis functions.

- The endpoints of a Bezier curve are defined by the endpoints of the control polygon. All other points on the curve are affected by all of the control points.

- Bezier curves are limited in that the number of control points determines the degree of the curve and they do not give you any local control.

- Joined Bezier curves are continuous if the endpoints match. They are C1 continuous if the last and first line segments of the control polygons are collinear.

- You can find the derivative of any point on a Bezier curve as a function of the derivatives of the basis functions.

CHAPTER 4

B-SPLINES

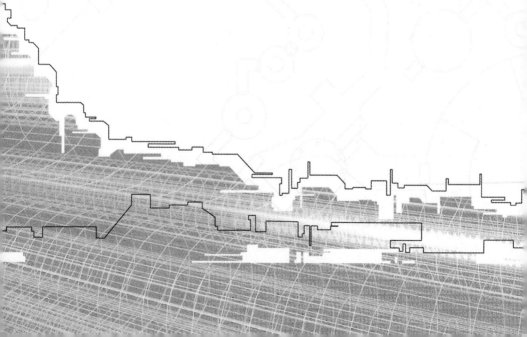

C hapter 3 introduced Bezier curves as an example of parametric curves that are based on a set of basis functions. Bezier curves are far more flexible than the polynomial curves discussed in Chapter 1, but they are still subject to many limitations. This chapter introduces B-splines (short for "basis" splines). These curves are also based on a set of basis functions, but they are far more flexible than Bezier curves. They are also more complicated, but I will show you some straightforward ways to deal with them based on the following topics:

- The building blocks of a B-spline
- Generating the basis functions
- Different types of knot vectors
- Controlling the parameters of a B-spline
- Closed B-splines
- Finding the derivatives of the basis functions
- Drawing B-splines

The Building Blocks of a B-Spline

As I said, B-splines are quite a bit more flexible than Bezier curves. This flexibility comes from the fact that you have much more control over the basis functions. Instead of being limited to the Bernstein basis functions, you can develop your own basis functions by controlling a handful of basic building blocks. Therefore, I will begin the explanation by deconstructing what you learned about polynomial and Bezier curves and add the new material needed for B-splines. Then, I show you how everything comes together to form the basis functions needed to draw these splines. I will begin with the control points.

Control Points

In this chapter, the way you manipulate the control points is largely the same as in Chapter 3. This is a set of points that controls the overall shape of the curve. The role of the basis functions will be to describe how points are interpolated between these control points. So, you can manipulate control points just like you did in Chapter 3. You can move them in two or three (or more) dimensions and rely on the basis functions to help change the resulting curve.

NOTE

All of the examples in this chapter deal with 2D curves. I do this because 2D is easier to visualize in figures. The concepts work exactly the same in three dimensions. The equations in this chapter apply to each component of the control point position, regardless of how many dimensions are used.

Having said that, there is a difference in the way that control points affect the curve. In Chapter 3, you saw that each control point had an effect on each point on the curve; likewise, the number of control points affected the degree of the curve. For the sake of flexibility, you would like to be able to arbitrarily set the degree of the curve and to also determine the range of effect each control point has. B-splines allow this level of control, but before I tell you how, I have to talk about what the degree of the curve really means.

Degree and Order

In Chapter 1, you learned that the highest exponent in the equation determined the degree of the polynomial curve. In Chapter 3, you saw that N control points yielded Bernstein basis functions of degree (N-1). So, N control points affected spans of curves with degree (N-1). In the case of Bezier curves, there was only one span, which was affected by all the control points.

At this point, I'd like to introduce some new nomenclature and talk about curves where the *order* is designated by k and the degree of the curve is (k-1). For example, each Bezier curve in Chapter 3 was fourth order with third-degree basis functions. The Bernstein polynomials are always (k-1) degree where k is always equal to N. B-splines and their basis functions are much more flexible.

B-splines decouple the number of control points (N) from the degree of the curve (k – 1) and the range of effect for the control points (k). In purely abstract terms, you can begin to think about curves in which each curve point is only affected by a subset of the control points instead of every control point (likewise, each control point only affects a subset of curve points). This is interesting because you now have more local control over the shape of the curve. You can talk about a curve of order k=4 with 16 control points. Moving one control point only affects a subset of the curve points as shown in Figure 4.1. The only way to do this with Bezier curves is to join several separate curves.

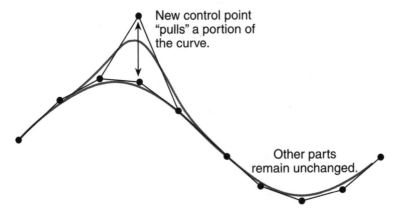

New control point "pulls" a portion of the curve.

Other parts remain unchanged.

Figure 4.1   *The advantages of local control.*

You can also think about curves of arbitrary degrees that are not fixed by the number of control points. Curves of higher degrees have spans that are influenced by more control points and are therefore smoother approximations of the control polygon. Curves of lower degrees have spans that are influenced by fewer control points and are therefore not as smooth. First degree curves degenerate into the control polygon, as show in Figure 4.2. The points on first degree curves are affected by two control points. Interpolating between two points is just a line, as shown in Chapter 3, "Parametric Equations and Bezier Curves."

So, you now have more control over the degree, but you don't have complete control. The order k determines the number of control points that affect subsets of curve points. Therefore, the maximum order of a curve is k=N, and the maximum degree of a curve is N-1. The minimum order is 2, which creates a first degree (linear) curve.

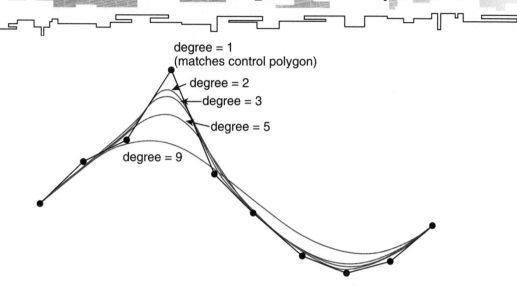

Figure 4.2   *Curves of various degrees.*

I have talked about order and degree in terms of how control points affect subsets or spans of curve points, but I have not yet told you how those spans are determined. With Bezier curves, you didn't have any mechanism to determine the subsets because the control points always affect every curve point. B-splines give you more control thanks to such a mechanism. This extra building block is called the knot vector.

Knot Vectors

The purpose of the knot vector is to describe the range of influence for each of the control points. Imagine you wanted to draw a third-order curve with five control points. Each control point affects some subset of curve points along the parametric range. You might describe the ranges of each control point as $[t_0, t_3]$, $[t_1, t_4]$, $[t_2, t_5]$, $[t_3, t_6]$, $[t_4, t_7]$. You could also compact this to a single sequence in the form of $[t_0\ t_1\ t_2\ t_3\ t_4\ t_5\ t_6\ t_7]$.

This is a knot vector. In this specific case, this knot vector could be used to describe how the control points influence a third-order curve with a parametric range of $t_0 < t\ t_7$. Figure 4.3 shows this more formally and shows how the ranges are encoded into the knot vector.

There are a couple of generalizations you can pull from this example. First, a knot vector must have $N + k$ elements. This is the number of elements needed to describe all of the ranges for each control point.

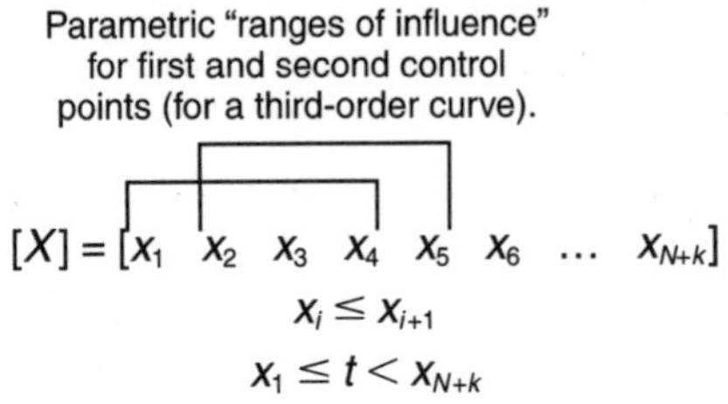

Parametric "ranges of influence"
for first and second control
points (for a third-order curve).

$$[X] = [x_1 \quad x_2 \quad x_3 \quad x_4 \quad x_5 \quad x_6 \quad \ldots \quad x_{N+k}]$$
$$x_i \le x_{i+1}$$
$$x_1 \le t < x_{N+k}$$

Figure 4.3 *A knot vector.*

Also, the elements of the knot vector must be monotonically increasing. This means that each subsequent element must be greater than or equal to the one before it. The actual values of the elements can either be monotonically increasing values on some arbitrary range, or they can be normalized to the range of [0,1]. These are three examples of knot vectors. Note that the second and third knot vectors are functionally equivalent. They would produce the same curve.

$$[X] = [3 \quad 4 \quad 5 \quad 6 \quad 7 \quad 8]$$
$$[X] = [1 \quad 2 \quad 3 \quad 4 \quad 5 \quad 6 \quad 7 \quad 8]$$
$$[X] = [0.125 \quad 0.25 \quad 0.375 \quad 0.5 \quad 0.625 \quad 0.75 \quad 0.875 \quad 1.0]$$

For most of the text explanations, I will use integer knot values as shown in the second knot vector above because it is a little bit easier to explain different knot vector types in those terms. In the code examples, I use normalized knot vectors because it makes it a little easier to think about different ranges where the parametric range is from 0 to 1. In either case, remember that there is no difference in the resulting curve.

There are two defined flavors of knot vectors labeled as uniform and nonuniform. The elements of a uniform knot vector are evenly spaced. In a nonuniform knot vector, they are not. The following are some examples of each flavor.

$$[X] = [1 \quad 2 \quad 3 \quad 4 \quad 5 \quad 6] \text{ (uniform)}$$
$$[X] = [1 \quad 3 \quad 5 \quad 7 \quad 9 \quad 11] \text{ (uniform)}$$
$$[X] = [1 \quad 2 \quad 2 \quad 3 \quad 3 \quad 4] \text{ (nonuniform)}$$
$$[X] = [1 \quad 2 \quad 3 \quad 3 \quad 4 \quad 5] \text{ (nonuniform)}$$

There are also two different types of knot vectors, open and periodic. I will describe the attributes and advantages of each type after I describe all of the building blocks. The full discussion of the knot vector is far from complete, but the specifics of different types of knot vectors will make more sense after you see how all the pieces come together.

At this point, you have all but one of the "building blocks". You know that a set of control points can be used to define a curve. You know that you can describe the properties of the curve in terms of the order and associated degree. You also have a mechanism (the knot vector) that allows you to talk about how the control points and the properties of the curve interact. You need one more basic building block—the piece that binds everything together and allows you to actually draw something—the basis function.

B-Spline Basis Functions

In Chapter 3, life was easier. Equation 3.7 gave you the Bernstein basis function solely as a function of the number of control points. Now, you have a lot more flexibility, but you also have a lot more to worry about. In addition to control points, the B-spline basis function must account for the degree of the curve, as well as the ranges defined by the knot vector. The resulting basis functions are defined not by Bernstein polynomials, but by the Cox-de Boor recursion formulas shown in Equation 4.1.

$$N_{i,1}(t) = \left\{ \begin{array}{l} 1 \text{ if } x_i \le t < x_{i+1} \\ 0 \text{ otherwise} \end{array} \right\}$$

$$N_{i,k}(t) = \frac{(t - x_i)N_{i,k-1}(t)}{x_{i+k-1} - x_i} + \frac{(x_{i+k} - t)N_{i+1,k-1}(t)}{x_{i+k} - x_{i+1}}$$

Equation 4.1   *Recursion formulas used to derive basis functions.*

The resulting basis functions are subject to the constraint that the sum of the basis functions must be equal to 1.0. In other words, see Equation 4.2.

$$\sum_{i=1}^{N} N_{i,k}(t) \equiv 1$$

Equation 4.2   *Constraint on the range of the basis functions.*

This constraint was always true for Bezier curves, but the flexibility of B-splines sometimes leaves cases where you must specifically account for this constraint. You will see why when I talk about periodic curves.

At first glance, these formulas can seem quite intimidating, but they aren't once you understand what they are doing. With Bezier curves, you used Equation 3.7 to derive a basis function. Now you must recursively find the basis functions for a given order, starting at the first-order basis functions. This is best described graphically, and by example.

Imagine I want to draw a fourth-order (k=4) cubic curve with 4 control points and I choose a knot vector of [X] = [0, 0, 0, 0, 1, 1, 1, 1]. Before I go any further, think about this knot vector in terms of Figure 4.3. I have created a knot vector that forces each control point to affect the entire curve. Sound familiar?

First, using the first part of Equation 4.1, I come up with the following first-order basis functions shown in Equation 4.3, which are shown graphically in Figure 4.4.

$N_{1,1} = 0$
$N_{2,1} = 0$
$N_{3,1} = 0$
$N_{4,1} = 1$

Equation 4.3   *First-order basis functions for*
k=4   [X] = [0   0   0   0 | | | |].

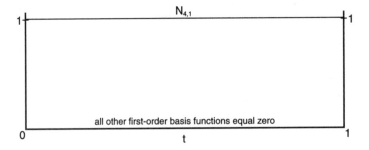

Figure 4.4   *First-order basis functions for*
k=4   [X] = [0   0   0   0 | | | |].

Those basis functions will now provide the input I need to define the second-order basis functions. This yields Equation 4.4, shown graphically in Figure 4.5.

$N_{1,2} = 0$

$N_{2,2} = 0$

$N_{3,2} = 1-t$

$N_{4,2} = t$

Equation 4.4   *Second-order basis functions for*
k=4, [X] = [0 0 0 0 1 1 1 1].

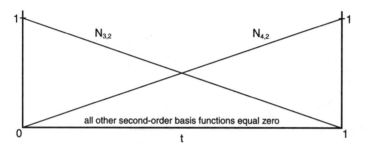

Figure 4.5   *Second-order basis functions for*
k=4, [X] = [0 0 0 0 1 1 1 1].

Repeating this for the third- and fourth-order basis functions, I get the following equations and graphs (Equations 4.5 and 4.6 and Figures 4.6 and 4.7).

$N_{1,3} = 0$

$N_{2,3} = (1-t)^2$

$N_{3,3} = 2t(1-t)$

$N_{4,3} = t^2$

Equation 4.5   *Third-order basis functions for*
k=4, [X] = [0 0 0 0 1 1 1 1].

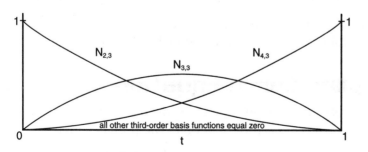

Figure 4.6   *Third-order basis functions for*
k=4, [X] = [0 0 0 0 1 1 1 1].

$$N_{1,4} = (1-t)^3$$
$$N_{2,4} = 3t(1-t)^2$$
$$N_{3,4} = 3t^2(1-t)$$
$$N_{4,4} = t^3$$

Equation 4.6 *Fourth-order basis functions for k=4, [X] = [0 0 0 0 1 1 1 1].*

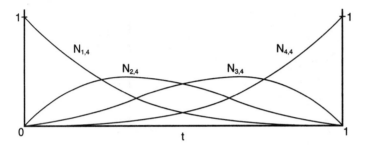

Figure 4.7 *Fourth-order basis functions for k=4, [X] = [0 0 0 0 1 1 1 1].*

The fourth-order basis functions are what you need for a fourth-order, third-degree curve. The graphs of these basis functions are shown in Figure 4.7. Look familiar?

As you can see, these basis functions are the Bernstein polynomials last seen in Chapter 3, when I mentioned that Bezier curves could be considered a special case of B-splines. Here is the proof. With the proper knot vector and degree, you can represent Bezier curves as a special case of the more general B-spline. The knot vector was chosen so that each control point affected the entire curve and the degree was chosen to match that of a Bezier curve with four points. I will talk about this in more depth when I talk about the different types of knot vectors.

These steps have walked you through all the components needed to draw your curve except for one very small and extremely important piece.

The B-Spline Curve Equation

You have a set of basis functions and you know the degree you want your curve to be. Equation 4.7 shows the equation of the B-spline curve.

This equation is extremely similar to the one given for Bezier curves. In this case, the set of basis functions to be used is determined by the

$$P(t) = \sum_{i=1}^{N} P_i N_{i,k}(t)$$

Equation 4.7 *B-spline curve equation.*

desired degree of the curve. The basis functions define the influence of each control point as a function of t. Once you have derived the necessary basis functions, the location of a point on the curve is simply a weighted sum of all the control points at a given value of t. Only now, the weight of some of the control points might be 0.

You now have the basic information about the building blocks you need to draw B-splines. So far, I have left out many of the details, most notably on the subject of the knot vector. Now that you have all the basic pieces, I will backtrack and fill in the details.

Knot Vectors

In the previous section, I mentioned that there are two types of knot vectors, open and periodic, and that there are two flavors, uniform and nonuniform. I will explain these in more detail and show the basis functions they yield. I'll only show the final basis functions of degree k, but you can derive the lower-degree functions if you want. Each of the illustrations is a screenshot from the source code developed for this chapter. At the end of the chapter, I'll explain how you can use the code to visualize basis functions of any degree.

Open knot vectors yield basis functions that are most similar to those seen in the last chapter, so I'll start with them.

Open Knot Vectors

Open knot vectors are characterized as having k repeated knot values at the beginning and end of the vector. The rest of the vector can be either uniform or nonuniform. Note that it is possible to have the repeated values at the ends and still be considered a uniform knot vector. Some examples are shown next.

k = 3   [X] = [0 0 0 1 2 3 3 3] (uniform)

k = 4   [X] = [0 0 0 0 1 1 1 1] (uniform)

k = 3   [X] = [0 0 0 1 1 2 2 2] (nonuniform)

k = 2   [X] = [0 0 1 2 3 3 3 4 5 6 6] (nonuniform)

Multiple knot values at the ends ensure that the first and last points on the curve correspond to the first and last control points. They essentially pull the curve ends to the ends of the control polygon. This happens because the duplicate values effectively constrain the ranges of the first

> **NOTE**
>
> The constraint given as Equation 4.2 will always be true when dealing with open knot vectors. You do not need to explicitly check for this.

and last control points and increase their relative influence within those ranges. This also ensures that the slopes at the ends of the curve equal the slopes of the first and last sides of the control polygon. This gives them the same end conditions as Bezier curves and makes them easier to join with other curves.

In the last section, I showed that Bezier curves were just a special case of B-splines by using an open knot vector. If you want to define a cubic B-spline with only four points and you want the end conditions given by an open knot vector, you might as well just use a Bezier curve. The advantage of B-splines is that you can have many more control points and keep the end conditions, but still set your degree to something reasonable. For example, a Bezier curve with ten control points would yield a tenth-degree curve. The knot vector for an equivalent B-spline would be

[X] = [0 0 0 0 0 0 0 0 0 0 1 1 1 1 1 1 1 1 1 1]

A B-spline with ten control points could yield a cubic curve (k = 4) with the following knot vector.

[X] = [0 0 0 0 1 2 3 4 5 6 6 6 6]

There are several advantages. You have control over the degree of the curve and you also have more local control. Figure 4.8 shows the Bezier equivalent curve (k = 10) and the cubic (k = 4) B-spline for the same set of ten control points. Notice the level of local control.

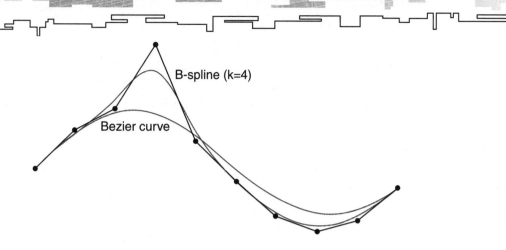

Figure 4.8 *Comparing Bezier and B-spline curves.*

The primary reason for choosing to use an open knot vector is the fact that you can pull the curve to the end points of the control polygon. This is good for joining curves and it makes it trivial to find the endpoints of the curve. But it can be a double-edged sword. Figure 4.9 shows the basis functions used to draw the B-spline in Figure 4.8.

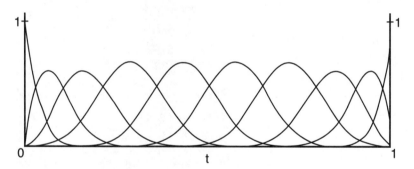

Figure 4.9 *Basis functions from Figure 4.8.*

As you can see, each basis function curve is a little different. This has ramifications when joining curves or when you create closed shapes with B-splines. In those cases, it may be advantageous to have a set of basis functions that are all similar.

Periodic Knot Vectors

In Chapter 2, "Trigonometric Functions," I introduced the idea of periodic functions like sine and cosine. Those functions are periodic because each individual wave can be thought of as a translation of the same basic sinusoidal wave. Knot vectors are periodic if they yield periodic basis functions. For example, the following uniform periodic knot vector (k = 4, N = 10) yields the periodic basis functions shown in Figure 4.10.

$$[X] = [1 \quad 2 \quad 3 \quad 4 \quad 5 \quad 6 \quad 7 \quad 8 \quad 9 \quad 10 \quad 11 \quad 12 \quad 13 \quad 14]$$

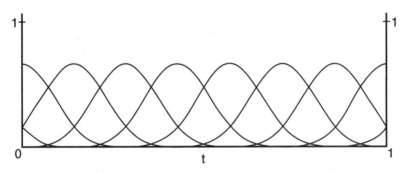

Figure 4.10 *Periodic basis functions.*

Periodic knot vectors do not necessarily need to be uniform. Figure 4.11 shows the periodic basis functions given by the following nonuniform periodic knot vector (k = 4, N = 4). Although it might be difficult to see in Figure 4.11, each basis function is the same shape as the other, only some are shifted so that you can only see a portion of them.

$$[X] = [0 \quad 1 \quad 2 \quad 3 \quad 6 \quad 7 \quad 8 \quad 9]$$

Figures 4.10 and 4.11 reveal a potential problem with periodic knot vectors. Look near the ends

> **NOTE**
>
> I don't take advantage of this in the sample code for this chapter, but the fact that the basis functions are all of the same shape could lead to optimizations when you are computing the basis functions. If they are all the same shape, why not compute one and translate it instead of computing all of them? I leave it to the highly motivated reader to optimize accordingly.

of the parametric ranges. The sums of the basis functions are not equal to 1.0, as dictated by Equation 4.2. This means that Equation 4.7 will not produce valid curve points for the entire range of [0, 9]. You need to find the reduced range for which Equation 4.2 is true. Generally, the usable parametric range for a knot vector that starts at 0 is

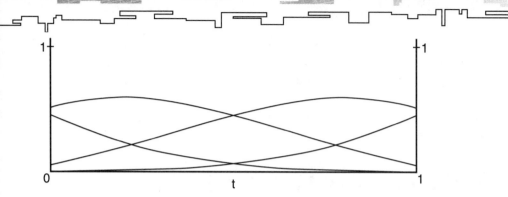

Figure 4.11   *Periodic basis functions.*

$[x_k, x_{N+1}]$. You can compute the reduced parametric range for a periodic knot vector with Equation 4.8.

$$3 \leq t < 6$$

Equation 4.8   *Parametric limits of the basis functions in Figure 4.12.*

Notice that the maximum value is less than 6 as opposed to less than or equal to 6. Once that is taken into account, the basis functions shown in Figure 4.11 produce the curve shown in Figure 4.12.

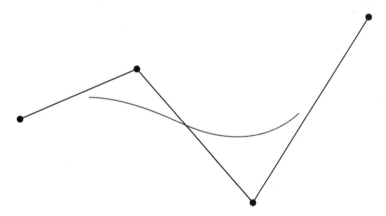

Figure 4.12   *B-spline curve based on a periodic knot vector.*

Figure 4.12 shows that the end points of the curve are nowhere near the endpoints of the control polygon. Also, the slope at the end of the curve is not the same as the slope of the last span of the control polygon. This could cause problems if you need to know where the end point is, but it does create interesting opportunities as well. I will address this again when I talk about closed shapes. There are ways to force the end points of a periodic curve to move to the end points of the control polygon (or anywhere else). Instead of talking about that specifically, this would be a good time to talk about spline manipulation in general.

Controlling the B-Spline

In the last chapter, the only way to control the shape of a Bezier curve was to move the control points. In this chapter, you have several ways to control the shape. I will walk through each one individually, but remember that you can manipulate all the controls at once to generate whatever effect you want.

Changing the Degree of the Curve

B-splines give you more control over the actual degree of the curve. A lower degree more closely approximates the control polygon. A higher-degree curve gives a smoother curve because it takes more of the control points into account. You can choose whatever degree you want, but remember that the number of elements in the knot vector also depends on the degree. Figure 4.13 shows three different curves with different degrees using the same control points. For the sake of simplicity, I have drawn them with open knot vectors. The three knot vectors are shown next.

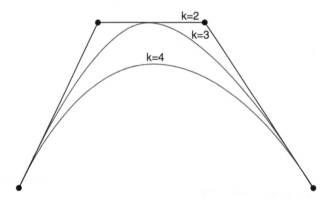

Figure 4.13   B-spline curves of varying degrees.

k = 2 [X] = [0 0 1 2 3 3]
k = 3 [X] = [0 0 0 1 2 2 2]
k = 4 [X] = [0 0 0 0 1 1 1 1]

As you can see, the curve becomes smoother as the degree gets higher.

Moving the Control Points

Moving the control points will move the points along the curve, but unlike Bezier curves, B-splines give you more local control. The locality of the control is determined by the degree of the curve. Figure 4.14 shows the effect of moving one of the control points first seen in Figure 4.13. Remember, the cubic curve behaves exactly like a Bezier curve in this specific case.

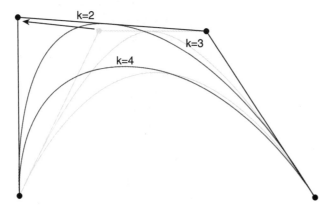

Figure 4.14   *Moving a control point of a B-spline.*

As you can see, the lower-degree curves give more local control. The fourth-order curve changes every point on the curve, just like a Bezier curve with four control points. However, I don't want to be misleading. You only lose localized control when k=N. Figure 4.15 shows another fourth-order curve with a total of ten control points. As you can see, the movement of the control point only affects a limited range of the complete curve.

Also, you can change the curve by adding control points. Unlike Bezier curves, you can add more control points without affecting the degree of the curve. This can be useful for "fine tuning" areas of the curve.

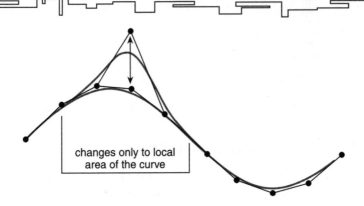

changes only to local
area of the curve

Figure 4.15   *Another example of local control.*

Duplicating Control Points

Equation 4.7 shows that the points along the curve are given as a
weighted sum of the effects of the control points. One of the ways you
can increase the relative influence of any given control point is to
create multiple control points in the same position. Every duplicated
control point will pull the curve closer to that position. Imagine you
have a curve and you want it to be very smooth in some parts and more
closely follow the control polygon in others. You have seen that the
degree of the curve sets the smoothness for the entire curve, but now
you have a case where you want one curve to have varying levels of
smoothness. You can accomplish this by setting the curve to a higher
degree and then duplicating the control points in the areas where you
want the curve to be less smooth. This is shown in Figure 4.16.

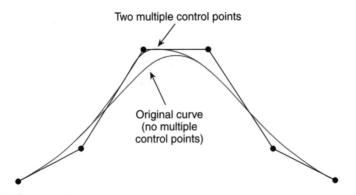

Two multiple control points

Original curve
(no multiple
control points)

Figure 4.16   *Duplicating control points.*

If you duplicate a control point k-1 times, the curve will be pulled all the way to the control point. This can be useful for creating sharp cusps in an otherwise smooth curve. You can also duplicate multiple control points to create linear segments in the curve. Both effects are shown in Figure 4.17.

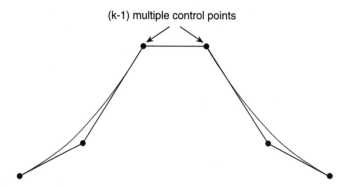

Figure 4.17 *The effects of k-1 duplications.*

It is worth noting that duplicate control points can be used to increase the overall parametric range of curves with periodic knot vectors. You can pull the end points of the curve to the end points of the control polygon if you have (k-1) multiple control points. This can be very useful if you need to know where the curve ends, but it does introduce a small linear segment that might or might not be advantageous. Figure 4.18 shows a periodic curve with multiple control points at the end points and also provides an open B-spline for comparison.

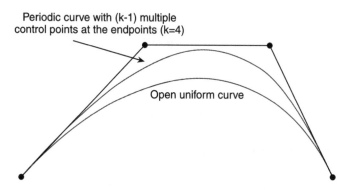

Figure 4.18 *Duplicating end points of periodic B-splines.*

Changing Knot Values

The final way that you can manipulate the curve is by manipulating the elements of the knot vector, generally creating nonuniform knots. Each element of the knot vector affects the range of influence of the control points. Figure 4.9 showed that duplicate knot values at the beginning and end of an open knot vector create basis functions that are equal to 1.0 at the beginning and end of the curve. This is what causes the curve to be pulled to the ends of the control polygon. The same effect can be created at other points along the curve by duplicating interior knot values. Figures 4.19 and 4.20 show examples of the basis functions formed with nonuniform knot vectors and their corresponding curves.

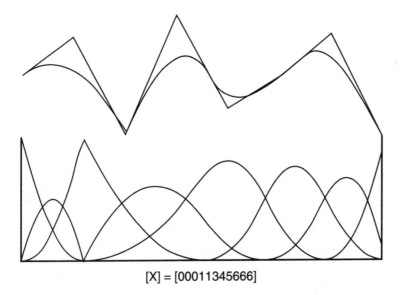

$$[X] = [00011345666]$$

Figure 4.19   *Basis functions and curve formed with a nonuniform knot vector.*

If a knot is repeated k times, the result will be a gap in the curve. However, this should be accounted for in the rendering technique. In this case, I am rendering the curve with a line strip, so the strip interpolates across any gaps. It might be useful in some circumstances to have gaps in the curve, but that would also force you to implement the curve with more vertices in a line list. Therefore, the formulation of a B-spline allows for gaps in the curve, but this particular rendering framework does not.

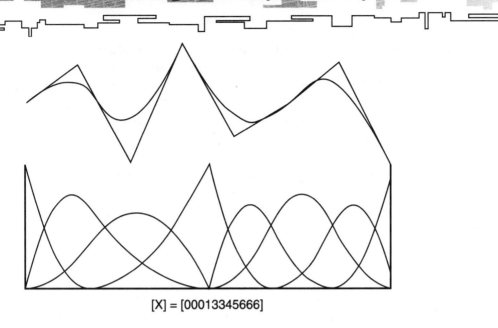

[X] = [00013345666]

Figure 4.20   *Basis functions and curve formed with a nonuniform knot vector.*

The effect of moving and duplicating knot vectors is not quite as intuitive as moving control points. Take some time to experiment with nonuniform knot vectors. Pay careful attention to how changes in the vector affect the relative shapes of the basis functions. After looking at that, see how those changes in the basis functions affect the shape of the curve itself. The code at the end of this chapter makes it very easy to make changes to a knot vector and visualize how those changes affect the shapes of the basis functions and the final curve. If you choose to, you could animate the knot values. In some cases, animation might make it easier to see what is actually happening.

Generating Closed Shapes with B-Splines

In addition to curves, it is also beneficial to talk about closed shapes. This will become especially important in the later chapters where I will be talking about three-dimensional objects created with parametric curves. In the present context of curves, a closed shape is simply a curve where the end points meet.

At first thought, this may seem like an easy problem to solve because you can just set the start and end point to the same position. Because of the behavior of a B-spline, this isn't exactly the case. Consider for a moment a curve created with an open knot vector. The end points of the curve are coincident with the end points of the control polygon. For the sake of creating a closed shape, this sounds perfect. However, there is a problem in that the slopes of the end of the curve match the slopes of the last span of the control polygon. That means you will have continuity problems where the two ends join. This is shown in Figure 4.21.

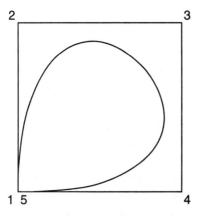

Figure 4.21   *Continuity issues with a closed shape.*

There are times where the kink you see in Figure 4.21 might be exactly what you need, but in many cases you will want a smooth shape. This would be very difficult with an open knot vector because of the way the slopes of the end points work out.

Look at how the basis functions of the two ends match up. Figure 4.22 shows the set of basis functions for the curve repeated so that the curve continues into itself. Speaking strictly in terms of the shapes, you

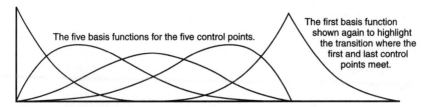

Figure 4.22   *Relationships between repeated basis functions.*

can see that the joined ends of the curve do not follow the same pattern as the rest of the basis functions.

I point out the relationships between the shapes of the basis functions because you do have an option where the shapes of the basis functions follow a repeating pattern. A periodic knot vector has continuity properties that are very useful for joining the ends by virtue of the periodicity of the basis functions.

Having said that, once you move to periodic knot vectors, you lose the convenience of the curve beginning and ending with the ends of the control polygon. As Figure 4.23 shows, a closed control polygon does not equal a closed shape.

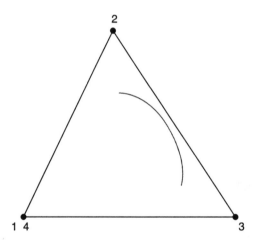

Figure 4.23 *Incomplete shape from a periodic knot vector.*

It turns out that there is an easy fix for this. You can complete the shape by adding (k-2) control points around the control polygon. This will pull the ends together, giving you a complete shape with smooth continuity. An example is shown in Figure 4.24.

Once you have set up the proper control points, you can manipulate the shape just like you would any other curve. Just remember to

NOTE

Figure 4.24 shows a triangle as the simplest closed shape. It is a coincidence that (k-2) more control points is also one more complete trip around the triangle. I don't want to give the false impression that all closed shapes require a second complete set of control points. The requirement is (k-2) extra control points.

move the coincident control points equally to avoid breaking the closed shape. In the next chapter, I will show a slightly different method of producing shapes and later I will show how to use these 2D shapes to build 3D objects.

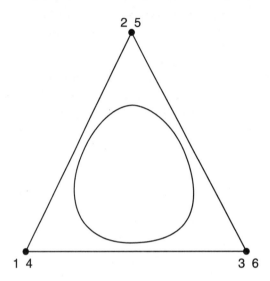

Figure 4.24 *Closing the shape with more control points.*

Finding Derivatives of B-Spline Curves

Finding the derivative of a point on a B-spline is conceptually the same as finding the derivative on a Bezier curve. You must first find the derivatives of the basis functions. Finding the derivative of Equation 4.1 is slightly more involved and requires more calculus than what I have given you in Appendix A. If you do apply a little more calculus, you get the derivative shown in Equation 4.9.

$$\frac{dN_{i,k}}{dt} = \frac{N_{i,k-1}(t) + (t - x_i)\dfrac{dN_{i,k-1}}{dt}}{x_{i+k-1} - x_i} + \frac{(x_{i+k} - t)\dfrac{dN_{i+1,k-1}(t)}{dt} - N_{i+1,k-1}(t)}{x_{i+k} - x_{i+1}}$$

Equation 4.9 *Recursive equation for the derivative of a basis function.*

Using this new equation, you can solve for the derivatives of a curve the same way you solve for points along the curve. The derivatives of the first-order basis functions are zero for all values of t, so you can use that to begin the recursive calculations at the second-order functions. The code needed to visualize the slope of the curve is included with all of the sample applications.

Up to this point, I have talked about this mathematically or in the abstract. It now seems like a great time to talk about the actual implementation.

Implementing B-Spline Code

Before I get into the code, I need to issue a word of warning. The following code was designed to be far more transparent than efficient. My primary concern was communicating the procedures and not in communicating tight, modular code. Therefore, there are five different projects for this chapter. They all share the same basic code, but each one is tweaked to demonstrate a different facet of this chapter. I decided it was far better to do this than to supply you with one monolithic application with several switches or cryptic options. As you read this, remember that most of this code could be collapsed into one tighter application.

Figure 4.25 shows a screenshot from the open uniform curve application. Almost all of the figures in this chapter were generated using these applications, but Figure 4.25 shows what the application looks like with all the drawing features enabled (control polygon, curve, slope indicator, and basis functions).

Having said that, I'll begin with the code found in \Code\Chapter04 – Open Uniform B Splines. This code serves as the foundation for the other applications. The basic structure can be seen in BsplineApplication.h.

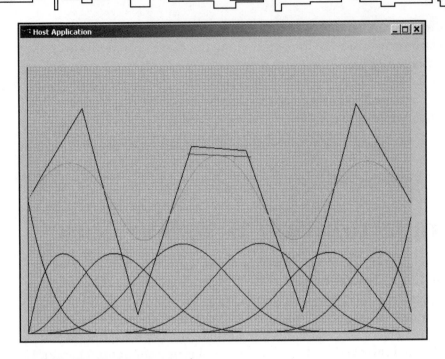

Figure 4.25   *Application screenshot.*

The Open Uniform B-Spline Application

```
#include "CurveApplication.h"
```

These settings define the number of control points and the curve order. You can change these numbers and recompile to see the effects of different orders. I have not added error checking to ensure that the order is less than or equal to the number of control points; keep that in mind as you experiment.

```
#define NUM_CONTROL_POINTS 6
#define CURVE_ORDER        4
```

Here I define the number of vertices along the curve.

```
#define NUM_CURVE_VERTICES   100

class CBSplineApplication : public CCurveApplication
{
public:
```

These functions define the building blocks of the curve. First, you set the knot vector elements and then generate the basis functions. `FillCurveBuffer` is called every frame to generate new curve points from moving control points.

```
void SetKnotVector();
void DefineBasisFunctions();
BOOL FillCurveBuffer();
```

These three functions draw the curve. The `Render` function draws the curve. You also have the option of calling the other two functions from `Render` if you'd like to see the basis functions and the slope.

```
virtual void Render();
void DrawBasisFunctions();
void DrawSlope();
```

The knot vector stores a set of normalized knot values in the range of 0.0 to 1.0. The exact values in the knot vector will depend on the type of curve you want to draw.

```
float        m_KnotVector[NUM_CONTROL_POINTS + CURVE_ORDER];
```

Instead of deriving the basis functions symbolically and then solving them for every value of t, I recursively evaluate a basis function for every value of t and use the array of precomputed values to create the curve. The following arrays hold those values. You can think of these arrays as holding the values that make up the basis function curves that you've seen throughout this chapter. There is a set of values for each basis function for each order. This takes up more memory than is absolutely necessary for rendering, but it makes it very easy to inspect what is actually happening with each recursive computation. The first array holds the actual basis values. The second array holds the slope at each of those points. You will see how these values are actually computed when I talk about `DefineBasisFunctions`.

```
float        m_BasisFunctions[NUM_CURVE_VERTICES]
                             [NUM_CONTROL_POINTS]
                             [CURVE_ORDER];

float        m_DerivativeBasis[NUM_CURVE_VERTICES]
                              [NUM_CONTROL_POINTS]
                              [CURVE_ORDER];
```

This is a vertex buffer that holds the computed curve points. It must be refilled every time the control points are moved.

```
LPDIRECT3DVERTEXBUFFER8 m_pCurveVertices;
};
```

The actual implementation of these functions can be found in \Code\Chapter4 – Open Uniform B Splines\BsplineApplication.cpp. As usual, the basic setup occurs in PostInitialize. Here, I create a vertex buffer that is large enough to hold the control points, the curve vertices, and the two end points of the slope line.

```
BOOL CBSplineApplication::PostInitialize()
{
        CCurveApplication::PostInitialize();

        if (FAILED(m_pD3DDevice->CreateVertexBuffer(
          (NUM_CONTROL_POINTS + NUM_CURVE_VERTICES + 2) *
sizeof(GENERAL_VERTEX),
                D3DUSAGE_WRITEONLY | D3DUSAGE_DYNAMIC, D3DFVF_GENERALVERTEX,
                D3DPOOL_DEFAULT, &m_pCurveVertices)))
                    return FALSE;
```

For this application, I define the knot vector once and compute the basis functions only once. These precomputed values can be used regardless of the position of the control points. They remain valid as long as you don't change the knot values.

```
        SetKnotVector();
        DefineBasisFunctions();

        return TRUE;
}
```

SetKnotVector does exactly that. In this case, it sets the knot vector values to create an open uniform knot vector. The values are normalized, so the vector will begin with k zeros, end with k ones, and contain evenly spaced fractional values in between.

```
void CBSplineApplication::SetKnotVector()
{
        int KnotValue = 0;
        for (long i = 0; i < CURVE_ORDER + NUM_CONTROL_POINTS; i++)
        {
```

```
        if (i <= NUM_CONTROL_POINTS && i >= CURVE_ORDER)
            KnotValue++;

        m_KnotVector[i] = (float)KnotValue /
                         (float)(NUM_CONTROL_POINTS -
CURVE_ORDER + 1);
        }
    }
```

DefineBasisFunctions is the most important new function. It applies the equations shown earlier in this chapter and evaluates the basis functions for a set of parametric values. As you walk through the code, keep in mind the fact that all of the equations were given with element indices beginning at 1. In code, arrays begin at 0, so I have to account for that when I index into the arrays.

```
void CBSplineApplication::DefineBasisFunctions()
{
```

First, I set all of the values in the array of derivative values to zero. I could get by with only setting the first-order values to zero, but I decided to go with a clean slate.

```
    memset(m_DerivativeBasis, 0,
        NUM_CURVE_VERTICES * NUM_CONTROL_POINTS *
        CURVE_ORDER * sizeof(float));
```

This is where things get interesting. I loop through the array of parametric values, setting the evaluated basis value as I move along. Remember, these arrays do not store the final curve positions. Instead, they store the values of the basis functions for each value of t. In this case, I create an evenly spaced set of values from t = 0.0 to t = 1.0.

```
    for (long Vertex = 0; Vertex < NUM_CURVE_VERTICES; Vertex++)
    {
```

This is where I set evenly spaced parametric values. You could choose different values. Perhaps you want to create more points along a given section of the curve and less in other sections. This is where you'd make those decisions.

```
        float t = (float)Vertex / (float)NUM_CURVE_VERTICES;
```

Now, loop through the first-order basis functions for each of the control points and apply the first step shown in Equation 4.1.

```
for (long ControlPoint = 0;
     ControlPoint < NUM_CONTROL_POINTS;
     ControlPoint++)
{
    if (t >= m_KnotVector[ControlPoint] &&
        t < m_KnotVector[ControlPoint + 1])
            m_BasisFunctions[Vertex][ControlPoint][0] = 1.0f;
    else
            m_BasisFunctions[Vertex][ControlPoint][0] = 0.0f;

}

}
```

At this point, you will have the values for the first-order basis functions.
The values will be either zero or one. If you plotted the values, the
graph would look something like Figure 4.4. Now that you have the
first order, you can recursively solve for the higher-order values by
looping through the orders and applying the second part of Equation
4.1. Loop through the order, the control points, and the parametric
values.

```
for (long Order = 1; Order < CURVE_ORDER; Order++)
{
    for (long ControlPoint = 0;
         ControlPoint < NUM_CONTROL_POINTS;
         ControlPoint++)
    {
        for (long Vertex = 0;
             Vertex < NUM_CURVE_VERTICES;
             Vertex++)
        {
```

I repeatedly define t. It can be argued that perhaps I should have set
the values of t in an array so that I only had to define them once.
That's a good idea, but I keep redefining them so that it is clear where
they come from.

```
float t = (float)Vertex / (float)NUM_CURVE_VERTICES;
```

These are my cryptically named variables that represent the elements of
Equations 4.1 and 4.9. The name Nikm1 stands for $N_{i,k-1}$ and so on. These
values should have been set by previous iterations through the loops.

```
float Nikm1    = m_BasisFunctions[Vertex]
                 [ControlPoint][Order - 1];
float Nip1km1 = m_BasisFunctions[Vertex]
                 [ControlPoint + 1][Order - 1];
float Dikm1    = m_DerivativeBasis[Vertex]
                 [ControlPoint][Order - 1];
float Dip1km1 = m_DerivativeBasis[Vertex]
                 [ControlPoint + 1][Order - 1];
```

These variables are elements of the knot vector. The variable names
follow the same pattern described above. In some cases, I have added
one to the array index. This is to account for the fact that the index
values in Equation 4.1 are one based and these arrays are zero based.

```
float xi     = m_KnotVector[ControlPoint];
float xikm1 = m_KnotVector[ControlPoint +
                           Order - 1 + 1];
float xik    = m_KnotVector[ControlPoint +
                           Order + 1];
float xip1   = m_KnotVector[ControlPoint + 1];
```

Now I have all the pieces, so I need to solve the equations. In doing so,
I handle the special case where I set $0/0$ equal to 0. I find the first and
second terms of both the basis function and the derivative.

```
float FirstTermBasis;
float FirstTermDerivative;
if (fabs(xikm1 - xi) < EPSILON)
{
        FirstTermBasis       = 0.0f;
        FirstTermDerivative = 0.0f;
}
else
{
        FirstTermBasis       = ((t - xi) * Nikm1) /
                               (xikm1 - xi);
        FirstTermDerivative = (Nikm1 + ((t - xi) *
                               Dikm1)) / (xikm1 - xi);
}

float SecondTermBasis;
```

```
              float SecondTermDerivative;
              if (fabs(xik - xip1) < EPSILON)
              {
                     SecondTermBasis      = 0.0f;
                     SecondTermDerivative = 0.0f;
              }
              else
              {
                     SecondTermBasis = ((xik - t) * Nip1km1) /
                                         (xik - xip1);
                     SecondTermDerivative = (((xik - t) * Dip1km1)
                                             - Nip1km1) /
                                             (xik - xip1);

              }
```

Now I add the two terms. The array now contains a precomputed basis function value for each value of t.

```
                     m_BasisFunctions[Vertex][ControlPoint][Order]   =
                                     FirstTermBasis + SecondTermBasis;
                     m_DerivativeBasis[Vertex][ControlPoint][Order] =
                                     FirstTermDerivative +
                                     SecondTermDerivative;
              }
          }
       }
}
```

FillCurveBuffer is called when the application wants to move the control points and recompute the curve. In this case, I call FillCurveBuffer every frame. As usual, I begin by locking the vertex buffer.

```
BOOL CBSplineApplication::FillCurveBuffer()
{
       if (!m_pCurveVertices)
              return FALSE;

       GENERAL_VERTEX *pVertices;

       if (FAILED(m_pCurveVertices->Lock(0,
```

```
        (NUM_CONTROL_POINTS + NUM_CURVE_VERTICES + 2) *
        sizeof(GENERAL_VERTEX),
        (BYTE **)&pVertices, D3DLOCK_DISCARD)))
            return FALSE;


    memset(pVertices, 0,
    (NUM_CONTROL_POINTS + NUM_CURVE_VERTICES + 2) *
    sizeof(GENERAL_VERTEX));
```

My method of moving the control points runs on autopilot. This loop runs through each control point and animates it in a sinusoidal pattern. In a real application, you would probably move the control points according to mouse input, collisions, and so on. In those cases, you would only refill the curve buffer when the control points actually moved.

```
    for (long ControlPoint = 0;
        ControlPoint < NUM_CONTROL_POINTS;
        ControlPoint++)
    {
        pVertices[ControlPoint].x = (600.0f /
        (float)(NUM_CONTROL_POINTS -
                            1) * (float)ControlPoint);
        pVertices[ControlPoint].y = 200.0f +
                            ANIMATE(200.0f *
                            sin(pVertices[ControlPoint].x));
        pVertices[ControlPoint].z = 1.0f;
        pVertices[ControlPoint].color = 0xFF000000;
    }
```

Now that the control point vertices are set, their values can be used in Equation 4.7. This loop computes the value of each point along the curve based on the control points and the basis function values.

```
    for (long i = NUM_CONTROL_POINTS;
        i < NUM_CURVE_VERTICES + NUM_CONTROL_POINTS;
        i++)
    {
        for (ControlPoint = 0;
            ControlPoint < NUM_CONTROL_POINTS;
            ControlPoint++)
```

```
        {
                    pVertices[i].x += pVertices[ControlPoint].x *
                                      m_BasisFunctions[i -
                                      NUM_CONTROL_POINTS]
                                      [ControlPoint][CURVE_ORDER - 1];
                    pVertices[i].y += pVertices[ControlPoint].y *
                                      m_BasisFunctions[i -
                                      NUM_CONTROL_POINTS]
                                      [ControlPoint][CURVE_ORDER - 1];
                    pVertices[i].z = 1.0f;
                    pVertices[i].color = 0xFFFF0000;
        }
    }
```

I have removed the second half of the function for brevity. The same
looping procedure is applied using the basis function derivative values
to find the slope at a given point on the curve. The code is very similar
to the slope-finding code seen in previous chapters.

Once all the vertices are set, the buffer is unlocked and they are ready
to be drawn.

```
        m_pCurveVertices->Unlock();

        return TRUE;
}
```

DrawBasisFunctions is an extremely inefficient utility function. I wanted
it to be self-contained so that it could be removed easily. As a result, it
inefficiently re-creates a vertex buffer every time it draws.

```
void CBSplineApplication::DrawBasisFunctions()
{
        LPDIRECT3DVERTEXBUFFER8 pBasisVertices;

        if (FAILED(m_pD3DDevice->CreateVertexBuffer(
                        NUM_CURVE_VERTICES * sizeof(GENERAL_VERTEX),
                        D3DUSAGE_WRITEONLY | D3DUSAGE_DYNAMIC,
                        D3DFVF_GENERALVERTEX,
                        D3DPOOL_DEFAULT, &pBasisVertices)))
            return;

        GENERAL_VERTEX *pVertices;
```

In this case, looping through the control points is actually looping through the different basis functions. The control points are not used when plotting the basis functions. The code locks and draws each function separately.

```
for (long ControlPoint = 0;
        ControlPoint < NUM_CONTROL_POINTS;
        ControlPoint++)
{
        if (FAILED(pBasisVertices->Lock(0,
                NUM_CURVE_VERTICES * sizeof(GENERAL_VERTEX),
                (BYTE **)&pVertices, D3DLOCK_DISCARD)))
            return;

        for (long x = 0; x < NUM_CURVE_VERTICES; x++)
        {
```

This code assumes that the values of t are evenly spaced. This x position is based on this assumption. The value of the basis function falls somewhere within the range of 0 to 1. I scale that value by 200 so that you can easily see the shape of the curve. In its current form, this function plots the highest-order basis functions. You can change the code if you'd like to see the other basis functions.

```
        pVertices[x].x = x / (float)(NUM_CURVE_VERTICES - 1) *
                    600.0f;
        pVertices[x].y = 200.0f *
                    m_BasisFunctions[x]
                    [ControlPoint][CURVE_ORDER - 1];
        pVertices[x].z = 1.0f;
        pVertices[x].color = ControlPoint *
                    (0xffffffff / NUM_CONTROL_POINTS);
    }

    pBasisVertices->Unlock();
```

This is where each individual curve is plotted.

```
        m_pD3DDevice->SetStreamSource(0, pBasisVertices,
                    sizeof(GENERAL_VERTEX));
        m_pD3DDevice->DrawPrimitive(D3DPT_LINESTRIP, 0,
                    NUM_CURVE_VERTICES - 1);
```

```
      }

      m_pD3DDevice->SetStreamSource(0, NULL, 0);
      pBasisVertices->Release();
}
```

This is where the curve is actually rendered. `FillCurveBuffer` animates
the control points and recomputes the curve buffer. Once that is done,
this code renders the control polygon, the curve, and the slope line. In
its current form, this function also draws the basis functions. You can
comment out `DrawBasisFunctions` if you only want to see the curve.

```
void CBSplineApplication::Render()
{
      CCurveApplication::Render();

      FillCurveBuffer();

      m_pD3DDevice->SetStreamSource(0, m_pCurveVertices,
                                 sizeof(GENERAL_VERTEX));

      m_pD3DDevice->DrawPrimitive(D3DPT_LINESTRIP, 0,
      NUM_CONTROL_POINTS - 1);

      m_pD3DDevice->DrawPrimitive(D3DPT_LINESTRIP, NUM_CONTROL_POINTS,
                                 NUM_CURVE_VERTICES - 1);

      m_pD3DDevice->DrawPrimitive(D3DPT_LINESTRIP,
                         NUM_CONTROL_POINTS + NUM_CURVE_VERTICES, 1);

      DrawBasisFunctions();
}
```

The preceding code provides a foundation for the other example
programs. The code was used to create the curves shown in Figure 4.13.

For the remaining code snippets, I will highlight the differences only.
The full source code can be found on the CD.

The Open Nonuniform B-Spline Application

The code for open nonuniform curves can be found on the CD in the \Code\Chapter04 – Open Nonuniform B Splines\ directory. There is only one major change here. The SetKnotVector function is changed so that one of the knot vector values is animated.

```
void CBSplineApplication::SetKnotVector()
{
        int KnotValue = 0;
        for (long i = 0; i < CURVE_ORDER + NUM_CONTROL_POINTS; i++)
        {
                if (i <= NUM_CONTROL_POINTS && i >= CURVE_ORDER)
                        KnotValue++;

                m_KnotVector[i] = (float)KnotValue /
                                (float)(NUM_CONTROL_POINTS - CURVE_ORDER + 1);
        }
```

The knots are first set as in the previous application, but then the first "inner" knot is animated back and forth between the two surrounding knots. It must not leapfrog the other knots because that would break the rule that the knot values must be monotonically increasing.

```
        m_KnotVector[CURVE_ORDER + 1] += ANIMATE(1.0f /
                                (float)(NUM_CONTROL_POINTS +
                                CURVE_ORDER + 1));
}
```

Remember, the basis functions must be redefined whenever the knot vector changes. In this case, I have changed the render function so that the knot vector, the basis functions, and the vertices are updated with every frame. The result is an animated curve similar to the curves shown in Figures 4.19 and 4.20.

The Periodic Uniform B-Spline Application

There are two changes in this application. The first change is that the knot vector is periodic and uniform. The knot values are evenly spaced from 0 to 1.

```
void CBSplineApplication::SetKnotVector()
{
        for (long i = 0; i < NUM_CONTROL_POINTS + CURVE_ORDER; i++)
        {
                m_KnotVector[i] = (float)i / (float)(NUM_CONTROL_POINTS +
                                CURVE_ORDER);
        }
```

Once the knot values are computed, you must explicitly redefine the parametric range as shown in Equation 4.8. I have subtracted a very small amount from the maximum value to satisfy the less-than constraint shown in Equation 4.8.

```
        m_MinT = m_KnotVector[CURVE_ORDER - 1];
        m_MaxT = m_KnotVector[NUM_CONTROL_POINTS] - 0.00001f;
}
```

The new knot vector affects the computation of the basis functions in one minor but important way. The previous examples generated values of t in the range of 0 to 1. Now, you must account for the decreased parametric range. The following code is a snippet from DefineBasisFunctions. It generates a set of even-spaced parametric values in the new range.

```
        for (long Vertex = 0; Vertex < NUM_CURVE_VERTICES; Vertex++)
        {
                float t = m_MinT + ((m_MaxT - m_MinT) *
                        (float)Vertex / ((float)NUM_CURVE_VERTICES - 1.0f));
```

This method of generating values for t is used in both DefineBasisFunctions and DrawBasisFunctions. You can definitely restrict yourself to some smaller subset of values within that range, but you must not try to use values outside of that range.

The application generates curves like the one seen in Figure 4.12.

Generating Closed Shapes with an Open Knot Vector

The code is identical to the first application except that I explicitly set the five control points to create a closed shape. The following code snippet is taken from the updated FillCurveBuffer function.

```
pVertices[0].x = 0.0f;
pVertices[0].y = 0.0f;
pVertices[1].x = 0.0f;
pVertices[1].y = 200.0f;
pVertices[2].x = 200.0f + ANIMATE(200.0f);
pVertices[2].y = 200.0f;
pVertices[3].x = 200.0f;
pVertices[3].y = 0.0f;
pVertices[4].x = 0.0f;
pVertices[4].y = 0.0f;
```

The first and last control points match, closing the shape. I have chosen to animate one of the points just to show the effect on the closed shape. The result looks similar to the shape shown in Figure 4.21.

Generating Closed Shapes with a Periodic Knot Vector

The code used for a periodic shape is the same as that used to create a periodic curve. In this case, I have created a triangle with six control points. Four are needed to create the closed triangular control polygon and two (k-2) more are needed to actually close the resulting shape. The following code snippet is from FillCurveBuffer. Notice that the third and sixth points must be animated in the same way. Matching control points must be moved equally if you want the shape to stay closed.

```
pVertices[0].x = 0.0f;
pVertices[0].y = 0.0f;
pVertices[1].x = 200.0f;
pVertices[1].y = 400.0f;
pVertices[2].x = 400.0f + ANIMATE(200.0f);
pVertices[2].y = 0.0f;
pVertices[3].x = 0.0f;
pVertices[3].y = 0.0f;
pVertices[4].x = 200.0f;
pVertices[4].y = 400.0f;
pVertices[5].x = 400.0f + ANIMATE(200.0f);
pVertices[5].y = 0.0f;
```

The resulting closed shape is similar to the shape shown in Figure 4.24.

Each of these applications has been tweaked to demonstrate the individual concepts found in this chapter. Take some time to experiment with the code. Manipulate the curve by changing the degree, moving the control points, and changing the knot vector. You can use the code to get a better feel for how these effects really work.

In Conclusion...

This chapter has covered many topics, but many of the examples shown are just different flavors of the same basic ideas. If there are concepts you don't understand, try playing with the code to get a better idea of how things work. Take a look at the shape of the basis functions. See what happens when you break some of the constraints (like the range of periodic curves). I have tried to give you a sandbox to experiment with. The concepts found in this chapter permeate almost all of the remaining chapters in this book. Take the time to get a solid understanding before moving on.

As you experiment, here are some important points to keep in mind:

- B-splines are similar to Bezier curves in that they are computed using a set of basis functions. Unlike Bezier curves, B-spline basis functions give the programmer much flexibility.

- B-splines are not constrained to a specific order or degree. This gives the programmer more control over the overall smoothness of the curve. The only constraint is that the order must not be more than the number of control points.

- The knot vector defines the range of influence of the control points. It defines the shapes of the basis functions, which in turn define the relative effect of each of the control points at every point along the curve.

- B-spline basis functions can be found recursively based on the desired order and the knot vector. If you change the knot vector, you must recompute the basis function curves.

- The sum of the basis functions at a given value of t must equal zero. In some cases, you will need to limit your parametric range to conform to this rule.

- The curve equation for B-splines is very similar to the Bezier curve equation. It is the sum of the influence of each control

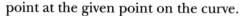

point at the given point on the curve.

- Knot vectors can be uniform and nonuniform. They can also be open or periodic.

- Open knot vectors have k multiple knots at either end of the vector. This has the effect of pulling the curve toward the end-points of the control polygon. The Bezier curve is a special case of an open B-spline.

- Periodic knot vectors produce periodic basis functions. Each basis function is the same shape as the other. This creates convenient continuity properties, but it limits the parametric range of the resulting curve.

- B-splines offer you more control over the shape of the curve. You can change the order/degree, move the control points, move the knot vector entries, and duplicate control points to produce a wide range of shapes and effects.

- Open knot vectors are not usually appropriate for closed shapes because of continuity problems at the joined endpoints.

- Periodic knot vectors are usually better for closed shapes, but they require (k-2) repeated control points in order to increase the parametric range and close the shape.

- Like Bezier curves, the derivative of a point on a B-spline is dependent on the derivatives of the basis functions.

- The code for this chapter was written for clarity rather than efficiency. It might be a useful exercise to create an optimized version. Tearing the code apart and putting it back together might help solidify the concepts.

CHAPTER 5

NURBS

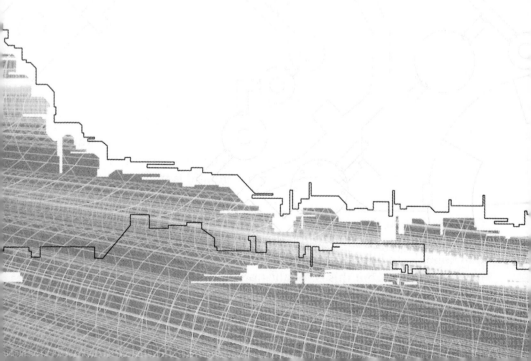

In Chapter 4, I introduced B-Splines, which can be treated as a
superset of the Bezier curves shown in Chapter 3. In this chapter, I
will talk about NURBS (Non-Uniform Rational B-Splines), which are a
superset of B-Splines. NURBS are extremely powerful and they are an
important feature in most modeling programs. It may seem paradoxi-
cal that this chapter is relatively short, but most of the important
groundwork was set in the previous chapter. In this chapter, I'll expand the material with the following concepts:

- Rational versus nonrational splines
- The effect of weighted control points
- Conic sections with NURBS
- Finding the derivative of a NURBS curve
- Drawing NURBS

NURBS: Rational Splines

NURBS is short for "Non Uniform Rational B-Spline". From the
previous chapters, you should be familiar with each of those terms
except for "rational". To define rational curves, I must first define
rational numbers. A number is rational if it can be represented as a
quotient of two integers. Most of the numbers you deal with on a daily
basis are rational numbers. For example, the number 5 can be represented as 5/1, 10/2, and so on. There are a few notable exceptions—
the most common one being pi. There are no two integers for which
the quotient equals pi. There are approximations, such as 22/7, but pi
cannot be exactly represented as a quotient and is therefore an irrational number.

Coming back to the context of curves, NURBS are defined as rational
curves because their basis functions are given as the quotients of two
polynomials. In light of this, the B-spline curves of Chapter 4 are
irrational curves, but this is usually not explicitly mentioned.

To understand where this quotient comes from, I need to again depart from curves for a moment. As a result of some of the mechanics of matrix operations, graphics equations are frequently expressed in terms of four-dimensional homogenous coordinates. In a homogenous coordinate system, XYZ points are usually given as XYZW coordinates during transformations. When they are projected back into 3D space, the new coordinates are given as (X/W, Y/W, Z/W).

If you define irrational B-splines in 4D space and then project them back into 3D space, you obtain NURBS with basis functions given by the following equation.

$$P(t) = \frac{\sum_{i=1}^{N} P_i W_i N_{i,k}(t)}{\sum_{i=1}^{N} W_i N_{i,k}(t)}$$

Equation 5.1 *Basis function for NURBS.*

In this equation, it usually makes the most sense to think of the W parameter as a "weight" for each control point. This is usually given as a homogenous coordinate vector or weight vector [W], similar to a knot vector. If you choose to, you can ignore the mathematical intricacies of rational numbers and homogenous coordinates and concentrate on the effects of a weighting factor for each control point. These weight factors have three main effects that offer advantages over the B-splines of Chapter 4.

First, unlike irrational B-splines, NURBS are invariant with respect to both affine and perspective transformations. B-splines are only invariant with respect to affine transformations (scaling, rotation, and translation). This means that you can perform perspective transformations on the control points and compute proper curve points with the transformed control points. This saves you the computational overhead of transforming every point along the curve. With hardware transformations, this may become less of an issue, but it can be an advantage.

Second, the ability to change the weighting factor of each control point gives you more control over the shape of the curve. In the previous chapter, I presented B-splines as a set of building blocks or controls that affected the shape of the curve. NURBS give you one more control, as you will see in the next section.

Finally, NURBS can be used to correctly draw conic sections such as circles. This can be extremely useful when drawing real-world shapes. I will go into more detail about conic sections later in this chapter.

These three factors make NURBS very effective as basic modeling primitives. In fact, programs like *Rhino3D* are almost entirely based on NURBS.

The Effects of Weighting Factors

In the previous chapter, I showed how the relative effect of each control point could be influenced by changes to the knot vector and/ or multiplicity of control points. In the case of the knot vector, changes had an effect on the range of influence for control points. In a given range, one control point might have more influence than the others due to a nonuniform knot vector.

Multiple control points were a crude way of affecting how the curve was pulled toward a given point. If all points have the same amount of "pull", doubling a control point effectively doubled its overall influence on the curve.

The addition of a weighting factor has a similar effect. If all the entries in the weight vector are set to 1, the result is the same as the B-splines seen in Chapter 4. Increasing the weights of control points relative to the others will give those points more pull on the curve, thereby influencing the shape of the curve. These effects are easiest to see when applied to a single control point. In the following examples, the curve is given with an open uniform knot vector (k=4) and the weight vector [1 1 w 1 1]. The next seven figures demonstrate the effect of changing the value of w.

Figures 5.1 and 5.2 show the curve and basis functions when w = 1. This curve is the same as an irrational B-spline (B-splines are just special cases of NURBS).

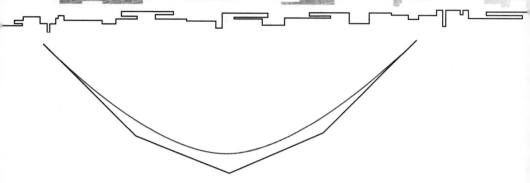

Figure 5.1 *B-spline from NURBS (w = 1).*

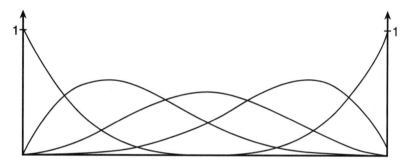

Figure 5.2 *Basis functions for Figure 5.1.*

In Figures 5.3 and 5.4, the value of w has been set to 0. If k=3, this would produce a straight line between the second and fourth control points. This wouldn't be surprising, because a weight of 0 would effectively remove the third control point from the equation. The third control point has no influence on the curve points in that range.

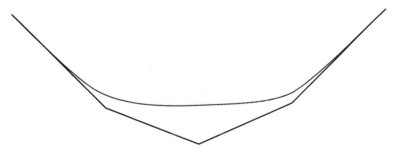

Figure 5.3 *Removing the influence of a control point (w = 0).*

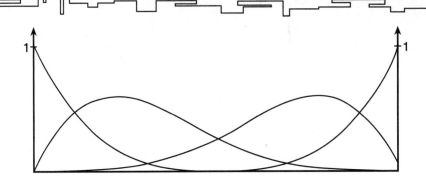

Figure 5.4 *Basis functions for Figure 5.3.*

The ability to dynamically "remove" the effects of control points or to create straight line segments could come in handy for some applications.

Figures 5.5 and 5.6 show what happens when w is set to some large number. As you can see, the relative influence of that point becomes much greater and the curve is pulled closer to that control point. In fact, the curve is pulled exactly to the control point when w equals infinity, but infinity is frequently an inconvenient value in code.

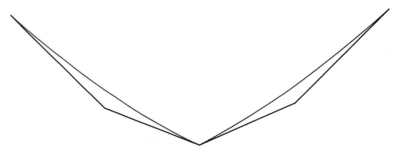

Figure 5.5 *Pulling a curve to a control point (w = 10).*

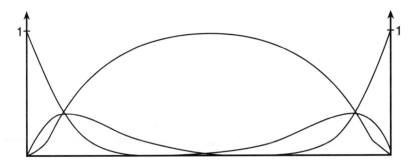

Figure 5.6 *Basis functions for Figure 5.5.*

Figure 5.6 shows that "heavier" basis functions "overpower" functions with lower weighting factors. This is something you should be mindful of.

Figure 5.7 shows several curves overlaid on top of each other with different values of w.

Each of these examples has been based on the same open uniform knot vector. The basic effect is the same for periodic knot vectors. The only difference is that, as Figures 5.4 and 5.6 show, the resulting basis functions will not be translates of each other if the relative weights are different. The "peaks" of the basis functions will be pulled higher as they are weighted.

> **NOTE**
>
> Mathematically speaking, the endpoints of an open curve should always correspond to the first and last control points. In practical terms, this might not be true if some weights are extremely high. Rounding errors in the basis functions or parametric values could cause a very high weight to pull an endpoint away from the last control point. For instance, the curve point at t=0.9999 might be pulled toward an extremely "heavy" interior control point. Be aware of this, even though you will probably not need to set weights to extremely high values.

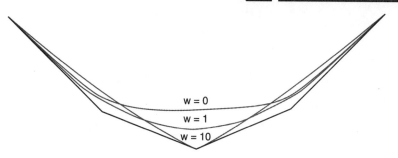

w = 0
w = 1
w = 10

Figure 5.7 *Several values of w.*

After you become familiar with the source code at the end of this chapter, explore the relative difference of different weighting factors on multiple control points, curves with k > 3, and different configurations. Also, try using negative weights. The basic structure of the source code is very similar to the code in Chapter 4.

As you will see in the source code, changes to the weight vector can be more computationally expensive than changes to the control points.

Therefore, you will probably want to make rough changes to the shape of the curve by moving the control points. You might find that changes to the weight vector are best suited for making very specific changes or specific shapes. One such specific case could be for drawing conic sections such as circles.

Conic Sections and NURBS Curves

Conic sections are the family of curves that are generated when a plane intersects a cone. Depending on the angle between the cone and the plane, the resulting intersection can be elliptical, parabolic, or hyperbolic, as shown in Figure 5.8.

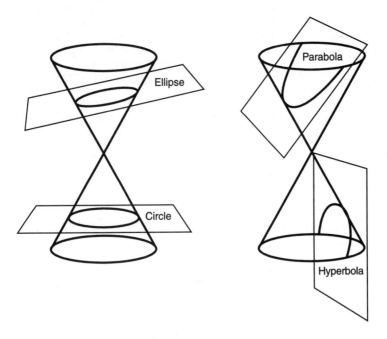

Figure 5.8 *Conic Sections.*

Most of the shapes shown in the previous chapters have been organic, free-flowing shapes. Organic shapes are useful, but it is also very useful to be able to draw shapes like circles (a special case of an ellipse). Unlike irrational B-splines, NURBS can be used to accurately represent conic sections.

Basic conic sections can be represented simply with quadratic (k=3) curves between three control points. The shape of the conic section is then determined by the relative weight of the middle control point. Figure 5.9 shows several different types of conic sections based on the same control points. The weight vector is [1 w 1].

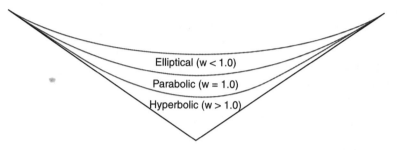

Elliptical (w < 1.0)

Parabolic (w = 1.0)

Hyperbolic (w > 1.0)

Figure 5.9 *Conic Sections from a quadratic curve.*

When w is 0, a straight line is drawn between the first and last control points. When w is between 0 and 1, the resulting curve is elliptical. When w equals 1, the curve is parabolic. For all values greater than 1, the resulting curve is hyperbolic.

For the remainder of this chapter, I will concentrate on circles because they are probably the most common conic section you will use. Circular arcs are special cases of ellipses, so you know the value of w will be some value between 0 and 1.

To find that value, imagine the three control points defining an isosceles triangle that encloses the arc of a circle, as shown in Figure 5.10.

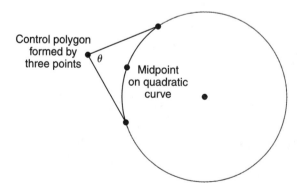

Control polygon formed by three points

θ

Midpoint on quadratic curve

Figure 5.10 *Defining an arc with an equilateral triangle.*

From Figure 5.10, you can see that you need to pick a value of w such that the midpoint of the curve falls on the circle. Based on this, you can apply Equation 5.1 and a bit of geometry and trigonometry to find w as a function of the angle theta. After jumping through a few trigonometric hoops, you will find Equation 5.2.

$$w = \cos\left(\frac{\theta}{2}\right)$$

Equation 5.2 *w as a function of the angle of the arc.*

As Figure 5.11 shows, the simplest way to draw a circle is with three sets of arcs—120 degrees each. The final circle has a knot vector [X] = [0 0 0 1 1 2 2 3 3 3] and a weight vector [W] = [1.0 0.5 1.0 0.5 1.0 0.5 1.0]. These knot values result from Equation 5.2 applied to 120 degree arcs.

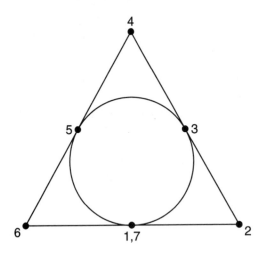

Figure 5.11 *Defining a circle with a triangle.*

A triangle might give you the simplest representation, but it gives you the fewest number of points to control. If you combine all the concepts seen so far, you can define the control points and weights in terms of the number of sides you want in the control polygon. This is demonstrated graphically in Figures 5.12 and 5.13.

There are 2N+1 control points. Each control point is positioned on the circle as described in Chapter 2. The radius used to compute the position of the circumscribed control points is shown to the right. N is the number of sides. In this case, N = 4.

The weight of each circumscribed control point is $\cos\left(\frac{4\pi}{N}\right)$

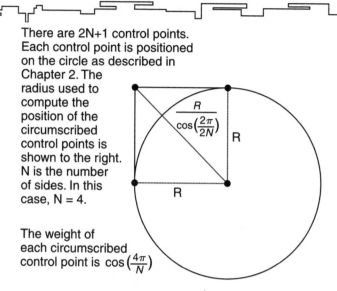

Figure 5.12 *Specifying circle controls in terms of the number of sides (N) of the control polygon.*

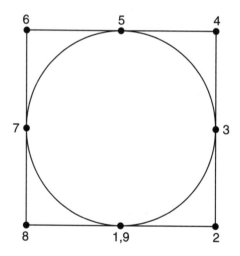

Figure 5.13 *Defining a square control polygon*
[X] = [0 0 0 1 1 2 2 3 3 4 4 4].

Once you can draw a circle, you can easily form an ellipse by moving the control points. You can also use a circle as a starting point for shapes that are symmetric about their center axis. Figure 5.14 shows how a circle can be used as a starting point for more interesting shapes.

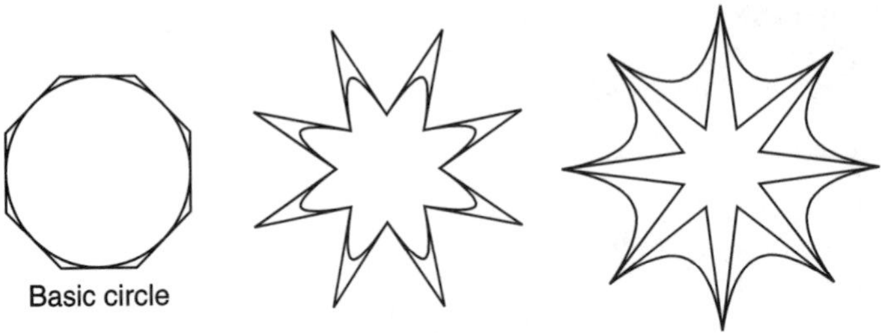

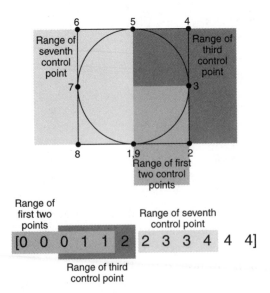

Basic circle

Control points moving inward and outward

Figure 5.14 *Moving the control points of a circle.*

Figures 5.11 and 5.13 are generated with the help of nonuniform knot vectors. Once you understand how to get the weighting factor for one of the segments, it is easy to see how to build a weight vector for several segments, but it may not be as easy to see how to build the concatenated knot vector. Remember that the knot vector defines the range of influence for each control point. With that in mind, I have supplied Figure 5.15 as a visual explanation of how a knot vector connects the individual arcs. Think of the knot values as quarters of the circle. The first two control points only influence the first quarter of the curve. The third and seventh control points affect the first and last half of the curve, respectively. If you have trouble figuring out what your knot vector should be, a diagram like Figure 5.15 can help.

Figure 5.15 *Explaining the concatenated knot vector.*

Once you understand how the knot vector (along with the order of the curve) affects the range of influence for each control point, it becomes very easy to generate curves that contain both conic sections and more organic shapes. Figure 5.16 shows such a curve. The last section of the curve is actually a quarter of a circle. I generated some random data for the first part of the curve, but I made sure to set the correct weight values, control point positions, and knot values for the circular section. The result is an erratic curve that ends with a smooth, mathematically correct circular arc.

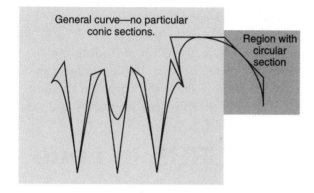

Figure 5.16   *Curve with conic section.*

The most important point to take away from Figure 5.16 is the fact that curves do not need to be strictly defined as one type or another. There are several labels defined here (uniform, open, conic). These labels are useful for talking about certain properties of curves, but they should not necessarily be seen as constraints. Use the combinations of knots, weights, degrees, and control points that make the most sense for a given situation.

Finding the Derivative of NURBS Curves

Finding the derivative at any point along a NURBS curve is conceptually the same as finding the derivative on a B-spline. Again, you must find the derivative of the curve with respect to t using the derivatives of the basis functions. For NURBS, the derivative of the basis functions is the following equation.

$$\frac{dP(t)}{dt} = \sum_{i=1}^{N} P_i \left(\frac{W_i \dfrac{dN_{i,k}}{dt}}{\displaystyle\sum_{i=1}^{N} W_i N_{i,k}} - \frac{W_i N_{i,k} \displaystyle\sum_{i=1}^{N} W_i \dfrac{dN_{i,k}}{dt}}{\left(\displaystyle\sum_{i=1}^{N} W_i N_{i,k}\right)^2} \right)$$

Equation 5.3　*The derivative of a NURBS basis function.*

Students of calculus will notice that this is the result of finding the derivative of Equation 5.1 using the quotient rule. This equation can be used to find the derivative of any point along the curve. In the next section, I will show you how to actually compute the derivative in code.

Implementing NURBS in Code

As I mentioned at the beginning of the chapter, the bulk of conceptual and implementation work for NURBS was done in the previous chapter. Therefore, I'm only going to give the new snippets here in the text. The full source code is available in the \Code\Chapter05 directories on the CD.

In NURBSApplication.h, you will see that the class has been augmented with several members that handle the weighting factors and new basis functions. As with all the source code, there are probably ways to make this code more efficient and less memory intensive, but this format is very clear. Note that the following code only includes the additions to the code.

The first additions are a weight vector and a function to set the weight values. This is very analogous to the knot vector and setting function seen in the previous chapter.

```
float m_Weights[NUM_CONTROL_POINTS];
void  SetWeights();
```

Next, I have added separate arrays for the weighted basis functions. You could limit the amount of memory used by folding the B-spline arrays and NURBS arrays together or by allocating only enough memory for the final order, but I have created a full duplicate in case you want to compare the basis functions.

```
float m_NURBSBasisFunctions[NUM_CURVE_VERTICES]
                          [NUM_CONTROL_POINTS]
                          [CURVE_ORDER];
float m_NURBSDerivativeBasis[NUM_CURVE_VERTICES]
                            [NUM_CONTROL_POINTS]
                            [CURVE_ORDER];
```

The weight vector is filled with the SetWeights function found in NURBSApplication.cpp. I have set up this function so that each weight is first set to 1.0. After that, you can individually set the weights of different control points as you see fit. The following code creates an animated weight for the third control point.

```
void CNURBSApplication::SetWeights()
{
        for (long i = 0; i < NUM_CONTROL_POINTS; i++)
                m_Weights[i] = 1.0f;

        m_Weights[2] = 10.0f * fabs(sin((float)GetTickCount() /
2000.0f));
}
```

Next comes the real meat of the code. The DefineBasisFunctions function has been augmented to create NURBS basis functions based on the B-spline functions seen in the last chapter. The function creates the array of B-spline basis values just as it did for the previous chapter, but it now includes one final step where the irrational basis functions, the weight vector, and Equations 5.1 and 5.3 are used to generate the NURBS basis functions and their derivatives. Again, you probably will only need the highest-order values, but I loop through all the orders here for the sake of completeness.

```
for (Order = 1; Order < CURVE_ORDER; Order++)
{
        for (long ControlPoint = 0; ControlPoint < NUM_CONTROL_POINTS;
             ControlPoint++)
        {
                for (long Vertex = 0; Vertex < NUM_CURVE_VERTICES;
                     Vertex++)
                {
```

As you loop through each order, control point, and parameter value, you can find the NURBS basis functions using Equations 5.1 and 5.3. The denominator of the basis function and the numerator of the second term of Equation 5.3 are both based on the sums of the products of the weights and irrational basis functions. Before computing the rational functions, you must first find those sums by looping through the irrational functions and multiplying them by the values in the weight vector.

```cpp
float Denominator = 0.0f;
float SumDerivatives = 0.0f;

for (long ControlWeight = 0;
     ControlWeight < NUM_CONTROL_POINTS; ControlWeight++)
{
        Denominator += m_Weights[ControlWeight] *
                       m_BasisFunctions[Vertex]
                       [ControlWeight][Order];
        SumDerivatives += m_Weights[ControlWeight] *
                          m_DerivativeBasis[Vertex]
                          [ControlWeight][Order];
}
```

Now that you have those sums, you can assemble the rational basis functions for both the curve and the derivative. The following code is the C++ implementation of Equations 5.1 and 5.3.

```cpp
m_NURBSBasisFunctions[Vertex][ControlPoint][Order] =
    m_Weights[ControlPoint] *
    m_BasisFunctions[Vertex][ControlPoint][Order] /
    Denominator;

m_NURBSDerivativeBasis[Vertex][ControlPoint][Order] =
    (m_Weights[ControlPoint] *
    m_DerivativeBasis[Vertex][ControlPoint][Order] /
    Denominator) -
    (m_Weights[ControlPoint] *
    m_BasisFunctions[Vertex][ControlPoint][Order] *
    SumDerivatives / (Denominator * Denominator));
```

```
        }
    }
}
```

Figure 5.17 shows a screenshot from the application found in the \Code\Chapter05 – NURBS with Open Uniform Knot Vector directory. I have enabled the basis function drawing functionality (DrawBasisFunctions now draws the NURBS values).

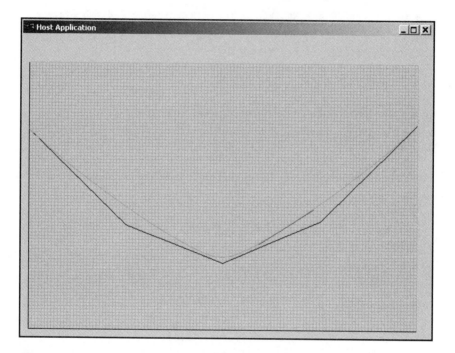

Figure 5.17   *Screenshot of basic NURBS application.*

I have also supplied two projects for drawing conic sections. The first one is very basic. It uses the preceding code, only this time the knot vector, weights, and control points are set to draw a circle with a triangle, as shown in Figure 5.11. The following snippets of code can be found in the \Code\Chapter05 – NURBS Conic Section 1 directory.

First, set the weights to match the values needed for a 120 degree arc.

```
void CNURBSApplication::SetWeights()
{
        for (long i = 0; i < NUM_CONTROL_POINTS; i++)
```

```
        m_Weights[i] = 1.0f;

    m_Weights[1] = m_Weights[3] = m_Weights[5] = 0.5f;
}
```

Now, set the knot vector needed to concatenate the three arcs.

```
void CNURBSApplication::SetKnotVector()
{
        m_KnotVector[0] = m_KnotVector[1] = m_KnotVector[2] = 0.0f;
        m_KnotVector[3] = m_KnotVector[4] = 0.333f;
        m_KnotVector[5] = m_KnotVector[6] = 0.666f;
        m_KnotVector[7] = m_KnotVector[8] = m_KnotVector[9] = 1.0f;
}
```

Finally, set the locations of the control points to draw a control polygon in the shape of an equilateral triangle. This code can be found in the DefineBasisFunctions function.

```
for (long ControlPoint = 0; ControlPoint < NUM_CONTROL_POINTS;
ControlPoint++)
{
        pVertices[ControlPoint].z = 1.0f;
        pVertices[ControlPoint].color = 0xFF000000;
}


pVertices[0].x = 300.0f; pVertices[0].y = 0.0f;
pVertices[1].x = 500.0f; pVertices[1].y = 0.0f;
pVertices[2].x = 400.0f; pVertices[2].y = 173.0f;
pVertices[3].x = 300.0f; pVertices[3].y = 346.0f;
pVertices[4].x = 200.0f; pVertices[4].y = 173.0f;
pVertices[5].x = 100.0f; pVertices[5].y = 0.0f;
pVertices[6].x = 300.0f; pVertices[6].y = 0.0f;
```

Figure 5.18 is a screenshot from this application including the basis functions.

This application was built with hardcoded values so that you could easily see the way a simple circle was built. The code found in \Code\Chapter05 – NURBS Conic Section 2 uses Equation 5.2 and the concepts from Figure 5.12 to create circles with an arbitrary number of sides.

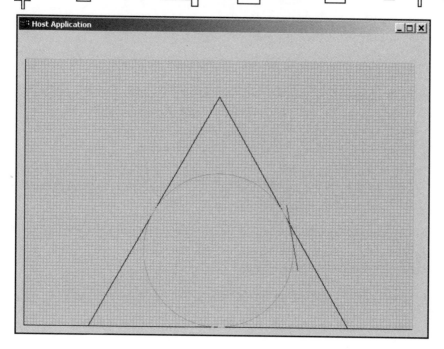

Figure 5.18   *Screenshot of basic conic section application.*

First, the weights are set. The odd control points represent the apex of each of the triangular subsections, so they must be weighted according to Equation 5.2. The even control points are given a weight of 1.0.

```
void CNURBSApplication::SetWeights()
{
        for (long i = 0; i < NUM_CONTROL_POINTS; i++)
        {
                if (i % 2)
                        m_Weights[i] = cos(TWO_PI / (float)NUM_SIDES / 2.0f);
                else
                        m_Weights[i] = 1.0f;
        }
}
```

Next, the concatenated knot vector is created. It is a nonuniform open knot vector created using the rationale seen in Figure 5.15.

```
void CNURBSApplication::SetKnotVector()
{
```

```
m_KnotVector[0] = m_KnotVector[1] = m_KnotVector[2] = 0.0f;

for (long i = 3; i < CURVE_ORDER + NUM_CONTROL_POINTS - 3; i += 2)
{
        m_KnotVector[i] = m_KnotVector[i + 1] =
                         (((float)i - 1.0f) / 2.0f) /
                         (float)NUM_SIDES;

}

m_KnotVector[i] = m_KnotVector[i + 1] = m_KnotVector[i + 2] = 1.0f;
}
```

Finally, the control points are set following the rationale shown in
Figure 5.12. The even points lie on the inscribed circle; the odd points
lie on the circumscribed polygon.

```
for (long ControlPoint = 0; ControlPoint < NUM_CONTROL_POINTS;
ControlPoint++)
{
        float Radius;
        if (ControlPoint % 2)
                Radius = 100.0f / cos(TWO_PI / (2.0f * (float)NUM_SIDES));
        else
                Radius = 100.0f;

        pVertices[ControlPoint].x = 300.0f + Radius *
                                        cos((float)ControlPoint * TWO_PI /
                                        (2.0f * (float)NUM_SIDES));
        pVertices[ControlPoint].y = 200.0f + Radius *
                                        sin((float)ControlPoint * TWO_PI /
                                        (2.0f * (float)NUM_SIDES));
        pVertices[ControlPoint].z = 1.0f;
        pVertices[ControlPoint].color = 0xFF000000;
}
```

Figure 5.19 shows a screenshot of a circle formed with an octagonal
control polygon. As the number of control points increases, you have
more freedom to create shapes such as those seen in Figure 5.14.

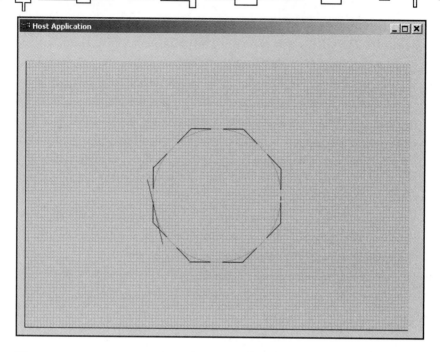

Figure 5.19   *Circle from an octagonal control polygon.*

In Conclusion...

In practical terms, rational curves are very similar to irrational curves. They are in fact a superset of irrational curves. The additional control given by the weighting factors can be extremely valuable and do not increase the overall complexity by that much. If you are serious about using splines, you will probably want to implement NURBS and treat B-splines and Bezier curves as special cases. In fact, in the next section on surfaces, I will only use Bezier and B-spline surfaces to explain the basics. After that, the other surfaces will be based on NURBS. Before moving to surfaces, here's a short review of the ideas in this chapter.

- NURBS are rational curves, meaning that their basis functions are quotients of two polynomials. In practical terms, this creates a weighting factor for each control point.

- NURBS are also invariant with respect to all transformations. This means that you could perform transformations on the control points and those transformations will be correctly propagated to the curve points. However, the advent of hardware transforms makes this difficult to exploit effectively.

- NURBS can be used to correctly represent conic sections. Therefore, NURBS can represent any shape, making them an extremely powerful modeling primitive.

- Weighting factors change the relative influence of a control point. A weight of zero will result in the point having no effect. A weight of infinity will pull the curve to that control point.

- Conic sections are the shapes you get if you slice a plane through a cone. I have concentrated on circles because you will often need to draw circles and because it's a good starting shape for many other things.

- You can build a circle from a series of quadratic curves with three control points each. The simplest form is a triangle with 120 degree arcs, but you can use as many as you need.

- You can find the derivative by finding the derivatives of the basis functions.

- The code for this chapter builds on the code from previous chapters. If you build a real application, you will probably want to make the code more efficient. You could divide DefineBasisFunctions into two functions that allow you to change the weighting factors without recomputing the entire basis function.

CHAPTER 6

SUBDIVISION OF CURVES

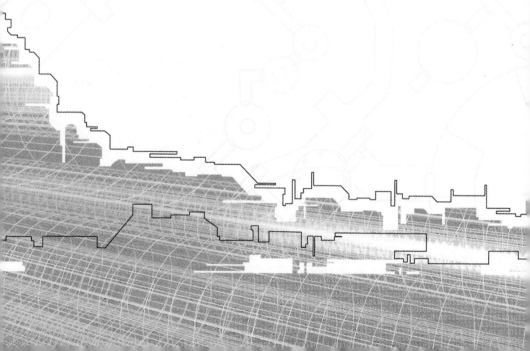

I n this final chapter of Part 2, I would like to introduce the topic of adaptive subdivision. In the previous chapters, curves were rendered using uniform subdivision. Each curve was made up of a number of line segments built with vertices spaced uniformly over the entire parametric interval. In areas where the curve is very flat, some vertices may be redundant. In areas with a lot of curvature, there might not be enough vertices to achieve a smooth curve. Adaptive subdivision is a method of placing vertices where they are needed most. The primary purpose of adaptive subdivision is to subdivide the curve at the drawing stage to produce more efficient rendering results while maintaining visual results. In general, this is advantageous for games because more efficiency means better performance. In this chapter, I will discuss the following topics.

- Simple adaptive subdivision for rendering curves
- A visual comparison between uniform and adaptive subdivision

Simple Adaptive Subdivision

Every example application so far has rendered curves using a uniform sampling of points along the curve to construct a set of lines that could be drawn using DirectX. This method is very simple to implement, but it can be very inefficient. Many times, too many points are used to draw straight regions. Often, too few points are used to draw curvy regions. This is shown in Figure 6.1.

In Figure 6.1, just as many points are used to draw the straight region as are used to draw the curved region. This is inefficient because the straight area is straight

> **NOTE**
>
> It is important to point out that there are several methods for curve subdivision. Each method has tradeoffs in terms of speed, efficiency, and accuracy. I have chosen to describe a method that places clarity above efficiency. Once you understand the basic ideas, you might want to investigate other methods.

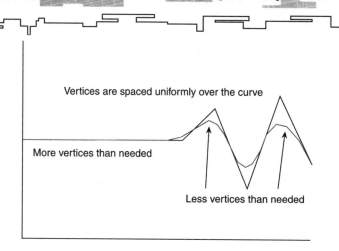

Figure 6.1   *Uniform sampling on a curve.*

with more points than it needs and the curved area has visible corners. Obviously, it would be better to redistribute the points to where they are most needed. This is the purpose of adaptive subdivision.

The word *subdivision* implies that you are dividing the curve into several small pieces. With uniform subdivision, I was dividing a curve into a predefined set of line segments of uniform (parametric) length. Adaptive subdivision means that the subdivision is based on decisions about where the curve actually requires more points. Those decisions require some analysis of the shape of the curve and a set of criteria that can be used to decide if an area needs to be subdivided further. To better understand the process, start with Figure 6.2.

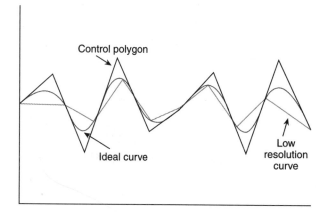

Figure 6.2   *Subdividing a curve.*

In Figure 6.2, the curve is rendered using as many vertices as there are control points. Unless the curve is very straight, this is probably the minimum number of vertices you'd ever use. There is another reason for this that you will see in a moment. Figure 6.2 shows both the very low-resolution curve and the ideal curve. The midpoint of each low-res line segment is compared to its counterpart on the ideal curve. Most subdivision schemes are based on the relationship between these two points. If the relationship passes some test, the line segment is used as is. Otherwise, it is split into two segments and the test is repeated on the two new line segments.

For this simple example, I have chosen to compare the distance between the two points to some tolerance factor. If the distance is greater than the tolerance value, another vertex is added at the ideal curve point. This is shown is Figure 6.3.

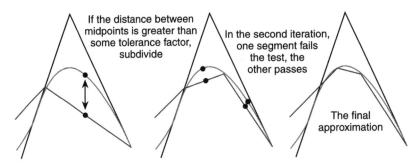

Figure 6.3 *Subdividing a curve by comparing midpoints.*

This process can be made to continue until either all segments pass the test or until the process exceeds a maximum number of vertices. Figure 6.4 shows one of the reasons why I started with more than one line segment.

In Figure 6.4, the one line segment would pass the midpoint test and never get subdivided. This is clearly incorrect and is a form of the aliasing effect shown in Chapter 2. Some subdivision schemes account for this more elegantly, but defaulting to a higher number of line segments is an easy way to start and will never produce aliasing errors.

In the spirit of this direct approach, the full diagram for the scheme I use in this book is shown in Figure 6.5.

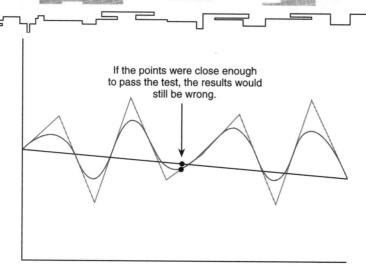

Figure 6.4 *Problem with too few segments.*

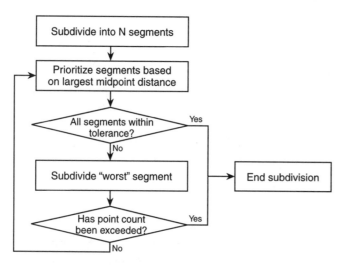

Figure 6.5 *The subdivision approach.*

This approach is slower than others because it sorts through the list of vertices each time and chooses the best case for subdivision. It might be slower, but it allows me to demonstrate several interesting features. If you knew that you only wanted to satisfy some tolerance value over all intervals, you could use an approach that linearly walks down the curve. The approach shown in Figure 6.5 is a simple way to subdivide based on the tolerance, a maximum number of vertices, or both. Also, the variable number of vertices has allowed me to demonstrate an alternate method of computing and setting the vertex positions.

The following section will highlight the code used for this subdivision scheme.

The Source Code

The CD includes the code for Chapter 6 in Code\Chapter06 – Subdivision. For simplicity, I have reverted back to using B-splines, but the method will work equally well for NURBS or Bezier curves. For the most part, it is based on the same underlying code seen in the previous chapters, but there are a couple of changes. The first change is that vertices are now stored as a linked list of points. This makes it easy to rearrange and add points while subdividing. This structure is called SD_VERTEX. It includes a parametric position, a screen position, and a pointer to the next vertex in the linked list.

```
typedef struct SD_VERTEX
{
       float t;
       float x, y;
       SD_VERTEX *pNextVertex;
} SD_VERTEX;
```

The class has been expanded to accommodate both the subdivision features. I only highlight the following new features.

```
class CBSplineApplication : public CCurveApplication
{
public:
```

These features support the subdivision scheme. m_pHead is the first vertex in the linked list. SubdivideCurve drives the subdivision process. GetPositionForT and FindBestCandidate are helper functions for the subdivision process. The first computes the actual curve point for a value of t and the second returns the line segment that needs subdivision the most. The source code for GetPositionForT is not shown in the text because it is very similar to the curve computation code shown in many of the previous chapters. The new application also keeps track of the number of resulting vertices.

```
       SD_VERTEX *m_pHead;
       void SubdivideCurve(long NumPoints, float Tolerance);
       void GetPositionForT(float t, float *pX, float *pY);
```

```
SD_VERTEX * FindBestCandidate(float Tolerance);
long m_NumVertices;
};
```

This is the code for adaptive subdivision (found in
BsplineApplication.cpp in the directory for this chapter).
SubdivideCurve drives the entire process.

```
void CBSplineApplication::SubdivideCurve(long NumPoints, float Tolerance)
{
```

First, clear out any old vertices that might be contained in the linked
list. This involves walking the list and deleting all of the members.

```
SD_VERTEX *pTemp;
while (m_pHead)
{
        pTemp = m_pHead;
        m_pHead = m_pHead->pNextVertex;
        delete pTemp;
}
```

Once the old values are gone, start with a uniformly divided set of
vertices based on the number of control points. Start by creating one
vertex at t = 0.0.

```
m_pHead = new SD_VERTEX;
m_pHead->t = 0.0f;
GetPositionForT(m_pHead->t, &(m_pHead->x), &(m_pHead->y));
SD_VERTEX *pCurrent = m_pHead;
```

Now, create the rest of the starter vertices. The overall process is very
similar to what you've seen in earlier chapters because I'm not
adaptively subdividing yet.

```
for (int i = 1; i < NUM_CONTROL_POINTS; i++)
{
        pCurrent->pNextVertex = new SD_VERTEX;
        pCurrent->pNextVertex->pNextVertex = NULL;

        pCurrent->pNextVertex->t = (float)i /
                                (float)(NUM_CONTROL_POINTS - 1);

        GetPositionForT(pCurrent->pNextVertex->t,
```

```
                    &(pCurrent->pNextVertex->x),
                    &(pCurrent->pNextVertex->y));

        pCurrent = pCurrent->pNextVertex;
    }
```

So far, you just have the starter points.

```
    m_NumVertices = NUM_CONTROL_POINTS;
```

Now it's time for the actual subdivision process. This loop continues
until either all tolerances are good or you have reached the maximum
number of points.

```
    while (TRUE)
    {
```

One of the inputs to this function is the maximum number of vertices
you want to create. If that many have been created, the loop stops. You
can force it to only pay attention to the tolerance constraint by setting
NumPoints extremely high.

```
        if (NumPoints && m_NumVertices == NumPoints)
                break;
```

Every time through the loop, the code picks the best line segment to
subdivide based on the midpoint distance comparison. If all segments
are within the tolerance, FindBestCandidate will return NULL.

```
        SD_VERTEX *pBest = FindBestCandidate(Tolerance);

        if (pBest)
        {
```

Subdivide the segment by creating a new vertex at the midpoint,
finding the real curve value at the midpoint, and inserting the new
point between the old ones. The fact that the real curve position is
computed in FindBestCandidate and then immediately recomputed here
presents at least one optimization opportunity.

```
            SD_VERTEX *pNew = new SD_VERTEX;
            pNew->t = pBest->t + (pBest->pNextVertex->t - pBest->t) /
                    2.0f;
            GetPositionForT(pNew->t, &(pNew->x), &(pNew->y));
            pNew->pNextVertex = pBest->pNextVertex;
```

```
            pBest->pNextVertex = pNew;

            m_NumVertices++;
        }
        else
            break;
    }
}
```

This function makes use of `FindBestCandidate` and `GetPositionForT`, which are both shown next. `FindBestCandidate` returns a pointer to the starting vertex of the line segment that has the largest gap between the real and interpolated midpoints.

```
SD_VERTEX *CBSplineApplication::FindBestCandidate(float Tolerance)
{
        SD_VERTEX *pCurrent = m_pHead;

        SD_VERTEX *pBestCandidate = NULL;
        float       CurrentDistance = 0.0f;
        float tm;
        float xm, ym;
        float xi, yi;
        float Distance;
```

Walk through the entire set of vertices. You could add more sorting mechanisms to make this more efficient. I wanted to make sure that the curve material was not obscured by other code.

```
        while (pCurrent->pNextVertex)
        {
```

Find the parametric value in the middle of the two parametric values of the current line segment and find the position for that value.

```
            tm = pCurrent->t +
                (pCurrent->pNextVertex->t - pCurrent->t) / 2.0f;

            GetPositionForT(tm, &xm, &ym);
```

Find the interpolated midpoint of the line segment.

```
            xi = pCurrent->x +
                (pCurrent->pNextVertex->x - pCurrent->x) / 2.0f;
```

```
yi = pCurrent->y +
        (pCurrent->pNextVertex->y - pCurrent->y) / 2.0f;
```

Compute the distance between the two midpoints. If it's greater than the current maximum and greater than the tolerance, set this point to be the best candidate for subdivision and set the current maximum distance to this distance.

```
Distance = sqrt((xi - xm) * (xi - xm) + (yi - ym) * (yi - ym));
if (Distance > CurrentDistance && Distance > Tolerance)
{
        pBestCandidate = pCurrent;
        CurrentDistance = Distance;
}

    pCurrent = pCurrent->pNextVertex;
}
```

If all segments were within the tolerance, this value will be NULL. Otherwise, it will be a pointer to the endpoint of the worst line segment.

```
return pBestCandidate;
}
```

The final change is that the FillCurveBuffer function is very different. Now, the code copies the vertices created during the subdivision process. I have not included that code in the text, but you might want to make sure you look at it on the CD.

Performance Considerations

Figure 6.6 shows the advantage of using subdivision. One curve is rendered with 100 vertices, the other with 30. A curve with 50 vertices is virtually indistinguishable from the 100 vertex curve.

As you can see, it is possible to produce nearly 100% visual quality with 30% of the vertices (for this particular curve). This means that you are passing far fewer vertices to the GPU. The method itself is not the best in terms of performance, but that might not matter if you are not animating the curve. If you are animating the curve using a vertex shader, you might find that it is actually better to send a larger number

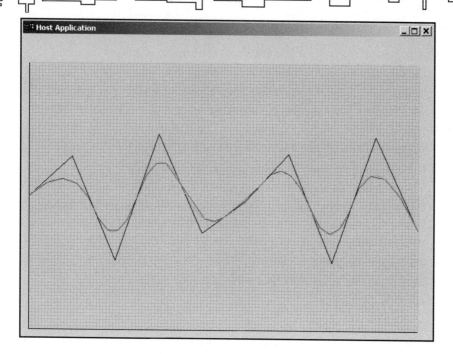

Figure 6.6   *The advantage of subdivision.*

of uniformly subdivided vertices. The reasoning is that a larger number of uniform vertices can approximate any shape during the animation. Inefficiencies caused by a larger number of vertices might be offset by the fact that you are not continually transferring data from the CPU. In cases like this, you can only really decide what's best after experimenting with all of the alternatives.

In Conclusion...

This chapter explained how to subdivide curves for more efficient rendering. As you can see in Figure 6.6, the process can make your curves much more efficient with a minimal loss of visual quality. The technique described here was very basic, but there are many papers and books that highlight different and faster methods. Once you understand the basic ideas, chances are you will find tweaks that directly address your needs.

This chapter concludes the material on simple 2D curves. Here are some of the points to remember:

- Adaptive subdivision is a method that approximates a curve based on some criteria about the shape of the curve.

- There are many types of tests that can be used to determine whether a curve should be subdivided at a given point. The method in this chapter measures the distance between the midpoint of a given line segment with the midpoint along that interval and compares it to some tolerance factor.

- The method described in this chapter supports subdivision based on a maximum number of segments, a tolerance factor, or both. You might want to spend some time experimenting with the parameters to see how the results change.

- Once you understand this method, a Web search will produce many others. It should be easy to find one that fits your specific needs.

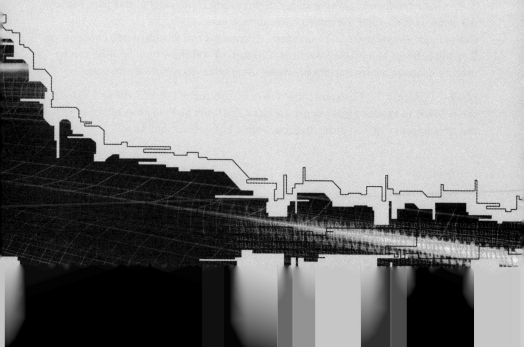

PART THREE

FOCUS ON
SURFACES

Curves are interesting and useful, but the most interesting 3D objects are built as collections of surfaces. In many cases, those surfaces are built with polygons with no explicit mathematical description. In this section, I will expand the previous curve concepts to surfaces and show how you can build complex shapes from simple and compact mathematical curves.

There are many advantages to a mathematical form. Much of this material was developed for CAD applications and fields like ship design where explicit shapes are an integral part of the design process. The idea of designing with a set of curves and shapes can also be useful for game developers when developing manmade shapes, such as cars and spaceships, or organic shapes, such as faces and trees. Another advantage is that these surfaces have a very compact representation. One mathematical surface can define the location of millions of vertices at several levels of detail. This can be very useful in an era of dynamic networked games and games with a very high amount of detail.

Although I cover several forms of surfaces, I do not cover subdivision surfaces. I chose not to address subdivision surfaces because there was no way to cover both NURBS and subdivision surfaces adequately in the space available. I chose to concentrate instead on NURBS because these representations provide a basis for subdivision surfaces at the mathematical level. If you have a solid understanding of how NURBS surfaces work, you will have an easier time with the mechanics of subdivision surfaces. Therefore, the material herein should prove useful no matter what type of surface you choose to use.

In Part 2, I introduced curves in order of increasing complexity. In this part, I follow the same path. Chapter 7 explains basic surface concepts in the context of relatively simple Bezier patches. From there, Chapters 8 and 9 apply those concepts to B-spline surfaces and NURBS surfaces. Chapter 10 will show how NURBS can be used to describe a wide variety of shapes using relatively simple constructs.

Finally, in Chapter 11, I'll explain how the new features of DirectX 8.1 and 9.0 can be used to render higher-order surfaces. You'll see how you can exploit the advantages of higher-order surfaces with a higher-level interface.

CHAPTER 7

BASIC SURFACE CONCEPTS AND BEZIER SURFACES

T he previous chapters introduced you to several forms of curves of increasing complexity. This chapter backtracks to Bezier curves in order to introduce some basic surface concepts using the simplest of the three previously discussed parametric forms. As you'll see, surfaces can be quite straightforward once you understand the basic curve concepts. This chapter will serve as a foundation for the next few chapters by introducing the following concepts.

- Extending curves to patch surfaces
- Finding the normal vector for a point on the surface
- Lighting a surface
- Using the simple 3D-viewing framework
- Setting up a basic 3D patch
- Implementing Bezier patches

Extending Curves to Patch Surfaces

In the previous curve chapters, you saw how to use a 1D parameter to control a 2D or 3D curve. Values of t moved you along a curve, and in the code examples, that curve consisted of a set of points on a 2D plane. Remember, the curves also work in 3D, but I limited them to 2D for clarity. This chapter introduces the idea of using a two-dimensional parametric space to control the shape of a 3D surface. The basic ideas shown in this chapter will apply to all surfaces.

NOTE
Parametric surfaces could also be 2D, but that is not usually very interesting. One case where it could be interesting is if you wanted to use the mathematics behind curves as the basis for 2D image warping and morphing.

As a point of reference, Figure 7.1 shows diagrams of 1D and 2D parametric spaces. The upper diagram shows the 1D space that I used for curves. In that case, the curve was controlled by one parameter, t. Movements through the 1D space resulted in movements along the curve. The lower diagram is the 2D space used for surfaces. In this case, I have defined the parameters as u and v. Movement within the 2D parametric space corresponds to movement along the 3D surface.

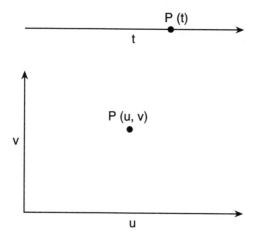

Figure 7.1 *Parametric spaces.*

This would be a good point to stress the difference between parametric space and the surface itself. Although the parametric space is 2D, you are not limited to 2D surfaces. Imagine you have a real 3D sheet of paper (this book contains roughly 150 of them). The surface of that sheet of paper defines a 2D parametric space, but each point on that surface is somewhere in 3D space. If you crumple the paper, the parametric value for a given point is the same, but the 3D position will change. Figure 7.2 shows that the same parametric point (u, v) can have different locations (x, y, z) depending on the state of the surface.

The point of Figures 7.1 and 7.2 is to show that surfaces are extremely similar to curves. With a curve, the 1D parameter t can define a point somewhere on that curve. With a surface, the 2D parameters u and v can define a point somewhere on the surface. Once you understand that, it is very easy to extend the curve ideas to surfaces.

Looking back to the previous chapters, each point on a curve is influenced by each control point. The basis functions determine the amount

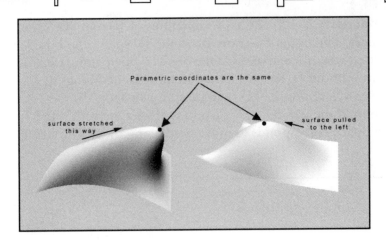

Figure 7.2 *Parametric points on a surface.*

of influence. In the case of surfaces, the same basic idea holds, only now control points in two dimensions exert influence on each point on the surface. The control points for a surface are now arranged in a control *grid*, as shown in Figure 7.3. In the case of Bezier surfaces, each control point affects each point on the surface for the same reasons that all the control points affect all the points on a Bezier curve.

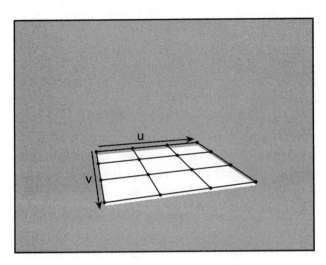

Figure 7.3 *Control grid for a parametric surface.*

The equation for surfaces is basically the same equation you saw for curves, only now you take into account the extra dimension. Equation 7.1 is the equation for Bezier surfaces.

$$P(u,v) = \sum_{i=0}^{N}\sum_{j=0}^{M} B_i(u)B_j(v)P_{i,j}$$

Equation 7.1 *Equation for Bezier surfaces.*

Notice the similarity with Equation 3.6. It looks a little more complicated, but it is essentially the same equation in two dimensions. Here
the contribution of each control point is scaled by two basis functions—one in each dimension. The Bernstein basis functions in this
case are exactly as described in Chapter 3, "Parametric Equations and
Bezier Curves," so I will not go over them again.

In short, both curves and surfaces are made up of a set of points. In
both cases, those points are computed as the weighted sums of the
influences of the control points. In the case of curves, those control
points existed in one parametric dimension—"along the curve". In the
case of surfaces, the control points exist in two parametric directions
on the surface. Conceptually, Equations 3.6 and 7.1 are basically the
same. The main difference is that the latter accounts for the second
parametric direction.

Finding Surface Normal Vectors

Each point on a surface has a normal vector that is perpendicular to
the surface at that point. These vectors are nearly as important as the
position because they really define how the surface will interact with
any other entity in the game world. For instance, the normal vector
defines how light will be reflected, refracted, or absorbed. The normal
vector also tells you the angle of the surface at that point. This can be
useful for terrain because you want objects to be correctly aligned as
they move over rolling hills. In this book, I will use the normal vector
for lighting calculations, both because it is extremely common and
because lighting helps you see the shape of the surface. When a
surface is a flat plane, it is very easy to conceptualize and compute the
normal vector. On a curved surface, it is slightly harder to do both, but
as you will see, you already have all the tools you need to do this.

If you have ever computed the normal vectors for vertices in a triangular mesh, you know that you can find a triangle's normal vector by taking the cross product of two of the edges. This process is shown in Figure 7.4. The cross product is discussed in Appendix B, "A Quick Look at Vectors."

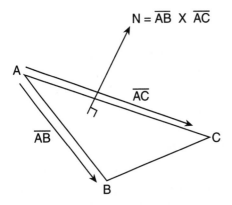

Figure 7.4 *Finding the normal vector of a triangle.*

For any two vectors, the cross product will give you a resulting vector that is perpendicular to both (assuming the first two are not parallel). Therefore, you can use the cross product to find the normal vector at any point on a surface if you know two vectors lie on the surface at that point. As luck would have it, you have two such vectors in the form of a tangent (slope) in the u direction and a tangent in the v direction. These two tangents are effectively the slopes as seen in previous chapters. Now, instead of dP/dt, you have dP/du and dP/dv. The cross product of these two vectors will give you the normal vector, but first you need to find the derivatives of Equation 7.1 with respect to u and v.

Appendix A ends with a very brief overview of partial derivatives. You might want to review that section if you haven't already. When you apply the concepts from Appendix A to Equation 7.1, you get the partial derivatives with respect to u and v as shown in Equation 7.2.

As usual, these equations are actually computed for each (x, y, z) component. Figure 7.5 shows the tangents on a surface. Notice that they are simply the slopes in the u and v directions. The grid is aligned such that u and v align with x and z so that the tangents are easier to visualize, but this is not a requirement. In Chapter 9, "NURBS Surfaces," you will see an example where the grid itself is more irregular.

$$\frac{dP}{du} = \sum_{i=0}^{N}\sum_{j=0}^{M}\frac{dB_i(u)}{du}B_j(v)P_{i,j}$$

$$\frac{dP}{dv} = \sum_{i=0}^{N}\sum_{j=0}^{M}B_i(u)\frac{dB_j(v)}{dv}P_{i,j}$$

Equation 7.2 *Derivatives with respect to u and v.*

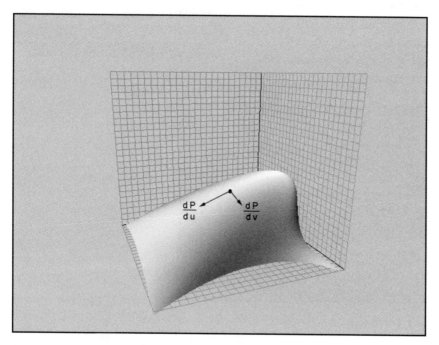

Figure 7.5 *Tangents on a surface.*

Equation 7.2 will give you two tangent vectors, but you still need to take the cross product if you want the normal vector. Equation 7.3 shows the final equation for the normal vector at any point on a Bezier surface.

$$N = \frac{dP}{dv} \times \frac{dP}{du}$$

Equation 7.3 *Computing the normal vector.*

Figure 7.6 shows the resulting normal vector.

Although Equations 7.2 and 7.3 focus on Bezier surfaces, the basic process of computing the normal vector for a surface will apply to all the surfaces shown in the coming chapters. As you have seen with curves, the basis functions change, but the underlying concepts remain the same. Equation 7.3 applies to all surfaces. Once you have computed the normal, you can apply basic lighting equations.

NOTE

When computing the normal vectors for vertices on a polygonal surface, it's best to average the normals of all the faces that share a particular vertex. In the case of parametric surfaces, you compute the normal vectors directly. There is no need to average them from polygons because you already have the mathematical definition of the surface.

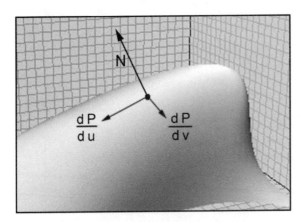

Figure 7.6 *Normal on a surface.*

Lighting a Surface

Once you have the normal vector, you could store that in a vertex and apply the standard DirectX lights. For this book, I have chosen not to do that for a couple of reasons. First, I wanted to limit the amount of DirectX specific code whenever possible. Second, I wanted to spend a brief amount of time showing you why the normal was important.

The examples in this book only deal with diffuse lighting. In this simple model, the intensity of reflected light anywhere on the surface is determined by the dot product of the normal vector and the opposite of the light direction, as shown in Figure 7.7. Both vectors should be normalized before computing the dot product.

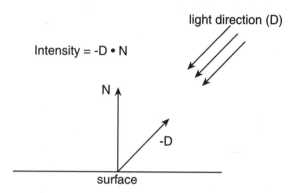

Figure 7.7 *Lighting on a surface.*

There are certainly more complex and realistic ways to light a surface, but this model is sufficient for these simple examples. In the source code, you will see this explicitly computed and placed into the vertex color. If you would rather light the surface with other methods, you could place the normal vector into the vertex and light the surface with a shader or fixed function lighting.

At this point, you have all the basic equations you need to render a Bezier surface. Before I show you the source code needed to actually implement these equations, I need to briefly go over the general 3D framework used in all of the surface chapters.

Extending the Basic Application to 3D

The previous chapters featured 2D curves drawn in a 2D environment. Now that I have moved onto 3D surfaces, I need to rework the application to be able to show these surfaces. Like most of the basic concepts in this chapter, this framework is not specific to Bezier surfaces and will remain the same for all surface examples.

The parent class for each of the surface examples is `CPatchApplication`, which replaces the 2D `CCurveApplication` used in previous chapters.

It sets up the World, View, and Projection matrices needed for 3D rendering and extends the grid to a full 3D box. Figure 7.8 shows a screenshot of the basic environment. The dimensions of the box were arbitrarily chosen to be 500 units on a side.

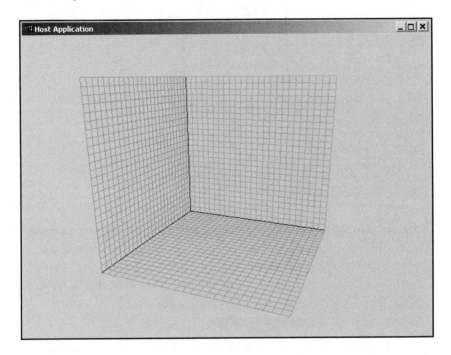

Figure 7.8   *The basic application environment.*

This class also has some basic controls for changing the viewpoint. The camera is always pointed at the center of the cube, but the left and right arrows rotate around the center. The up and down arrows increase and decrease the camera's height. I have tried to set up the application framework in a way that allows you to totally ignore the intricacies of the 3D environment (matrices, and so on), but you might want to experiment with different viewpoints or controls. Also, I have chosen movement values that work well on my system. If you find that the viewpoint changes too slow or too fast, you can alter the speed by changing the following values in PatchApplication.cpp in any of the surface projects.

```
#define HEIGHT_DELTA   20.0f
#define ORBIT_DELTA    0.1f
```

I have not included a full discussion of the code in the interest of space. If you are comfortable with 3D rendering in general, you will find that the code is very straightforward. If you are not comfortable, you can ignore the framework entirely and focus on rendering the surface.

Setting Up Buffers for a Generic Surface

There are a number of things that need to be set up before you can actually render a surface. The following points apply to all surfaces, so one could argue that they could have been pushed back into the basic framework, but I have chosen to explicitly expose them because they are important and not entirely trivial. The following code can be found on the CD in the directory \Code\Chapter07 – Bezier Patches\BezierPatchApplication.cpp, but it also appears unchanged in the source code for the later chapters as well.

Each surface in the examples is rendered as a set of lines showing the control grid and a set of triangles that form the actual shaded surface. With curves, I was able to get by with a simple line strip, but 3D rendering requires a bit more setup. First of all, I have created a set of values that define how many control points will be used and how many vertices should be created. These values will be used to determine the size of the vertex buffer.

These values determine the number of control points along the u and v directions. In the specific context of Bezier surfaces, they also determine the order of the surface. This is not necessarily the case with B-spline surfaces and NURBS surfaces.

```
#define NUM_U_POINTS 4
#define NUM_V_POINTS 4
```

These values determine how many vertices will be created in each direction. To simplify matters, the number of vertices is the same in both directions, but there is no constraint that forces you to do this. The number of triangles is based on the number of vertices. Two triangles are drawn between each set of four vertices, as shown in Figure 7.9.

```
#define NUM_PATCH_VERTICES 20
#define NUM_PATCH_TRIANGLES (2 * (NUM_PATCH_VERTICES - 1)*
                            (NUM_PATCH_VERTICES - 1))
```

9 vertices yield (3−1)*(3−1)*2 = 8 triangles

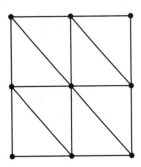

Figure 7.9   *Vertices and the resulting triangles.*

The vertex buffer will hold the control points and the vertices needed for the surface, so the total size of the buffer is the sum of the total number of control points and vertices.

```
#define NUM_TOTAL_VERTICES (NUM_U_POINTS * NUM_V_POINTS +
                    NUM_PATCH_VERTICES * NUM_PATCH_VERTICES)
```

For 3D rendering, indexed triangle lists and indexed line lists provide the best tradeoff between efficiency and simplicity. I use indexed line lists to render the control grid and indexed triangle lists to render the surface. To do that, I need to create an index buffer. The size of the buffer is determined by the following values.

```
#define NUM_GRID_INDICES  ((2 * NUM_U_POINTS * (NUM_V_POINTS - 1)) +
                    (2 * NUM_V_POINTS * (NUM_U_POINTS - 1)))
#define NUM_PATCH_INDICES (6 * NUM_PATCH_VERTICES * NUM_PATCH_VERTICES)
#define NUM_TOTAL_INDICES (NUM_GRID_INDICES + NUM_PATCH_INDICES)
```

The preceding macros should remain untouched for all of the surface chapters. However, you can change the number of control points by changing NUM_U_POINTS and NUM_V_POINTS. You can also increase or decrease the resolution of the surface by changing the value of NUM_PATCH_VERTICES. However, remember that the total number of vertices is the square of the value you set. Large values will result in slower rendering times.

Once the values are set, the vertex and index buffers are set up as shown next. Again, I am showing the code for CBezierPatchApplication, but the same code applies to all the surfaces.

```
BOOL CBezierPatchApplication::PostInitialize()
{
        CPatchApplication::PostInitialize();
```

First, I create a vertex buffer and index buffer for the total number of vertices and indices. The vertex buffer will not be filled until later, but the index buffer will be filled right away and will remain unchanged for the duration of the application.

```
        if (FAILED(m_pD3DDevice->CreateVertexBuffer(NUM_TOTAL_VERTICES *
                                    sizeof(GENERAL_VERTEX),
                                    D3DUSAGE_WRITEONLY |
                                    D3DUSAGE_DYNAMIC,
                                    D3DFVF_GENERALVERTEX,
                                    D3DPOOL_DEFAULT,
                                    &m_pPatchVertices)))
                return FALSE;

        if (FAILED(m_pD3DDevice->CreateIndexBuffer(NUM_TOTAL_INDICES *
                                    sizeof(short),
                                    D3DUSAGE_WRITEONLY,
                                    D3DFMT_INDEX16,
                                    D3DPOOL_DEFAULT,
                                    &m_pPatchIndex)))
                return FALSE;
```

Once the index buffer is created, lock the index buffer so that it can be filled.

```
        short *pIndices;
        m_pPatchIndex->Lock(0, NUM_TOTAL_INDICES * sizeof(short),
                        (BYTE**)&pIndices, 0);
```

This first loop creates the indices for the lines of the control grid in the v direction.

```
        for (long UIndex = 0; UIndex < NUM_U_POINTS; UIndex++)
        {
                for (long VIndex = 0; VIndex < NUM_V_POINTS - 1; VIndex++)
                {
                        *pIndices       = VIndex + (UIndex * NUM_V_POINTS);
```

```
                *(pIndices + 1) = VIndex + (UIndex * NUM_V_POINTS) + 1;

                pIndices = pIndices + 2;
        }
}
```

The second loop creates the indices for the lines of the control grid in
the u direction. When this loop is complete, the first part of the index
buffer will contain the values needed to draw the control grid with an
indexed line list. A line list allows you to draw all of the lines with a
single call to DrawIndexedPrimitive.

```
for (long VIndex = 0; VIndex < NUM_V_POINTS; VIndex++)
{
        for (long UIndex = 0; UIndex < NUM_U_POINTS - 1; UIndex++)
        {
                *pIndices        = VIndex + (UIndex * NUM_V_POINTS);
                *(pIndices + 1) = VIndex + ((UIndex + 1) * NUM_V_POINTS);

                pIndices = pIndices + 2;
        }
}
```

This final block of code sets up the indices for the indexed triangle
list. Notice that the index buffer contains indices for two types of
primitives. This is okay as long as you use the right indices at the right
time. Figure 7.10 shows how the index values are determined. For the
sake of simplicity, the preceding control point vertices are ignored.

These indices will apply equally well to any patch surface as long as
you are consistent with how you define the actual vertices. Remember, the index buffer is set up assuming that the vertex buffer is
arranged in a certain order. You will see how the vertex buffer is
filled later in the chapter.

```
for (UIndex = 0; UIndex < NUM_PATCH_VERTICES - 1; UIndex++)
{
        for (long VIndex = 0; VIndex < NUM_PATCH_VERTICES - 1; VIndex++)
        {
                *pIndices        = (NUM_U_POINTS * NUM_V_POINTS) +
                                   VIndex + (UIndex * NUM_PATCH_VERTICES);
```

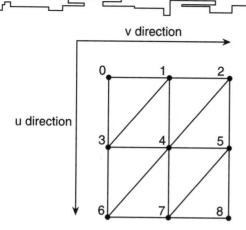

Index Buffer = {0, 1, 3, 1, 3, 4, 1, 2, 4, 2, 4, 5....}

Figure 7.10 *Making sense of the index buffer.*

```
            *(pIndices + 1) = (NUM_U_POINTS * NUM_V_POINTS) +
                              VIndex +
                              (UIndex * NUM_PATCH_VERTICES) + 1;
            *(pIndices + 2) = (NUM_U_POINTS * NUM_V_POINTS) +
                              VIndex +
                              ((UIndex + 1) * NUM_PATCH_VERTICES);
            *(pIndices + 3) = (NUM_U_POINTS * NUM_V_POINTS) +
                              VIndex +
                              (UIndex * NUM_PATCH_VERTICES) + 1;
            *(pIndices + 4) = (NUM_U_POINTS * NUM_V_POINTS) +
                              VIndex +
                              ((UIndex + 1) * NUM_PATCH_VERTICES);
            *(pIndices + 5) = (NUM_U_POINTS * NUM_V_POINTS) +
                              VIndex +
                              ((UIndex + 1) * NUM_PATCH_VERTICES) + 1;

            pIndices = pIndices + 6;
        }
    }
    m_pPatchIndex->Unlock();

    return TRUE;
}
```

There is one last piece of code that applies to every surface example. The Render function performs the actual drawing. For the most part, it is the same for every application.

```
void CBezierPatchApplication::Render()
{
```

Make sure you call the base class Render function if you want to render the grid lines. Also, the base class handles setting the FVF and other basic setup, so you probably don't want to remove this line without adding or rearranging the setup code.

```
        CPatchApplication::Render();
```

FillPatchBuffer computes the actual mesh. Each application implements FillPatchBuffer in its own way. The code for Bezier patches is described next.

```
        FillPatchBuffer();
```

Set the vertex and index buffers. Both buffers are used for the control grid and surface.

```
        m_pD3DDevice->SetStreamSource(0, m_pPatchVertices,
                                        sizeof(GENERAL_VERTEX));
        m_pD3DDevice->SetIndices(m_pPatchIndex, 0);
```

I have added a line that you can enable or disable if you want to draw the surface in wireframe mode. After that, you are ready to draw the surface. First, a call to DrawIndexedPrimitive renders the surface as an indexed triangle list. After that, the control grid is rendered as an indexed line list.

```
        //m_pD3DDevice->SetRenderState(D3DRS_FILLMODE, D3DFILL_WIREFRAME);
        m_pD3DDevice->DrawIndexedPrimitive(D3DPT_TRIANGLELIST, 0,
                                        NUM_TOTAL_VERTICES,
                                        NUM_GRID_INDICES,
                                        NUM_PATCH_TRIANGLES);
        m_pD3DDevice->DrawIndexedPrimitive(D3DPT_LINELIST, 0,
                                        (NUM_U_POINTS * NUM_V_POINTS),
                                        0, (NUM_GRID_INDICES / 2));
}
```

This completes the general code. As you can see, there is nothing included in the code that is specific to Bezier surfaces. The bulk of computation for each surface occurs in `FillPatchBuffer`.

The `FillPatchBuffer` function is where all of the magic happens; although, in the case of Bezier patches, the magic is fairly simple. This is really the first bit of source code that is not general to all the surface chapters. This implementation of `FillPatchBuffer` builds a Bezier surface based on a 4x4 control grid.

The function requires a set of basis functions and their derivatives. These are defined as macros at the top of BezierPatchApplication.cpp. Notice that I don't explicitly define separate basis functions for u and v because they are identical in this case. Therefore, I chose to keep t as the parameter for the macros to accentuate the fact that the basis functions are the same as seen in Chapter 3, "Parametric Equations and Bezier Curves."

```
#define B0(t) ((1.0f - t) * (1.0f - t) * (1.0f - t))
#define B1(t) (3.0f * t * (1.0f - t) * (1.0f - t))
#define B2(t) (3.0f * t * t * (1.0f - t))
#define B3(t) (t * t * t)

#define dB0(t) ((6.0f * t) - (3.0f * t * t) - 3.0f)
#define dB1(t) (3.0f - (12.0f * t) + (9.0f * t * t))
#define dB2(t) ((6.0f * t) - (9.0f * t * t))
#define dB3(t) (3.0f * t * t)
```

The macros are used to compute the vertex coordinates in the patch buffer.

```
BOOL CBezierPatchApplication::FillPatchBuffer()
{
```

The first several lines lock the vertex buffer as you've seen in previous chapters.

```
    if (!m_pPatchVertices)
            return FALSE;

    GENERAL_VERTEX *pVertices;
```

```
if (FAILED(m_pPatchVertices->Lock(0, NUM_TOTAL_VERTICES *
                                sizeof(GENERAL_VERTEX),
                                (BYTE **)&pVertices,
                                D3DLOCK_DISCARD)))
        return FALSE;
```

I start by positioning the control points in a uniform 4x4 grid at a
height of 100 units. Remember, these are the control points—not the
vertices that comprise the surface. You don't have to start out with a
uniform grid, but it makes things slightly clearer.

```
for (long U = 0; U < NUM_U_POINTS; U++)
{
        for (long V = 0; V < NUM_V_POINTS; V++)
        {
                pVertices[U * NUM_V_POINTS + V].x = U * (500.0f /
                                        (float)(NUM_U_POINTS - 1));
                pVertices[U * NUM_V_POINTS + V].y = 100.0f;
                pVertices[U * NUM_V_POINTS + V].z = V * (500.0f /
                                        (float)(NUM_V_POINTS - 1));
                pVertices[U * NUM_V_POINTS + V].color = 0xFF000000;
        }
}
```

I have also chosen to animate the heights of a few of the control
points. As you will see next, this code is tailored for a 4x4 control grid,
so it is fairly safe to use hardcoded indices. When you move on to the
next chapter, it might not be safe to make such assumptions because
you will be able to set arbitrary control grids.

```
pVertices[0].y = 100.0f + ANIMATE(100.0f);
pVertices[1].y = 100.0f + ANIMATE(100.0f);
pVertices[2].y = 100.0f + ANIMATE(100.0f);
pVertices[3].y = 100.0f + ANIMATE(100.0f);
pVertices[15].y = 200.0f + ANIMATE(200.0f);
pVertices[12].y = 200.0f + ANIMATE(200.0f);
```

You are not limited to changing the height of each control point. The
following code also changes the x coordinate, which will produce a wave
effect. In this case, I take the safer approach by finding the middle
control point as a function of the total number of control points.

```
long MidPoint = NUM_V_POINTS * NUM_U_POINTS / 2 + NUM_V_POINTS / 2;

pVertices[MidPoint].y = 500.0f;
pVertices[MidPoint].x = pVertices[MidPoint].x + ANIMATE(800.0f);
pVertices[MidPoint - 1].y = 500.0f;
pVertices[MidPoint - 1].x = pVertices[MidPoint - 1].x +
ANIMATE(800.0f);
```

Now I begin computing the vertices for the surface. Earlier, I said that
the basis functions are the same for both u and v. This is true, but the
result of those functions is different for different values of u and v.
Therefore, I have created two arrays to hold the evaluated basis function values. Two more arrays hold the evaluated derivatives needed for
the slope values.

```
float BU[4];
float BV[4];

float DU[4];
float DV[4];
```

These four variables will be used to compute the lighting intensity for
each vertex. The lighting code will be shown later, but notice the
direction of the light. In this case, I wanted the light to be shining
straight down. The intensity is based on the dot product of the normal
and the *opposite* of the light direction, so I set the vector to point
straight up.

```
D3DXVECTOR3 dPdU;
D3DXVECTOR3 dPdV;
D3DXVECTOR3 Normal;
D3DXVECTOR3 LightDirection(0.0f, 1.0f, 0.0f);
```

Now I'm ready to compute the vertex positions. The following nested
loop computes the values for each point on the surface. Remember
that the index buffer ordering is related to the order you compute
things here. If you change the order in which the vertices are computed, the resulting indexed surface might not be correct. Feel free to
change both, but remember that you cannot change one without
considering the effects on the other.

```
for (U = 0; U < NUM_PATCH_VERTICES; U++)
{
        for (long V = 0; V < NUM_PATCH_VERTICES; V++)
        {
```

The u and v values are uniformly distributed between 0 and 1 over the surface. Before any computation, you first need to know what the u and v values are.

```
float UVal = (float)U / (float)(NUM_PATCH_VERTICES - 1);
float VVal = (float)V / (float)(NUM_PATCH_VERTICES - 1);
```

The following code finds the values of all the basis functions at the u and v "positions". It also finds the values needed to compute the normal vector.

```
BU[0] = B0(UVal); BU[1] = B1(UVal);
BU[2] = B2(UVal); BU[3] = B3(UVal);

BV[0] = B0(VVal); BV[1] = B1(VVal);
BV[2] = B2(VVal); BV[3] = B3(VVal);

DU[0] = dB0(UVal); DU[1] = dB1(UVal);
DU[2] = dB2(UVal); DU[3] = dB3(UVal);

DV[0] = dB0(VVal); DV[1] = dB1(VVal);
DV[2] = dB2(VVal); DV[3] = dB3(VVal);
```

This code processes everything in two dimensions, but the vertex buffer is a one-dimensional array of vertices. This variable maps the 2D parametric value to its proper index in the array.

```
long Current = (NUM_U_POINTS * NUM_V_POINTS) +
               (U * NUM_PATCH_VERTICES) + V;
```

First, clear all the values to 0. This will make it slightly easier to compute the position as the sum of the influence of each control point.

```
pVertices[Current].x = 0.0f;
pVertices[Current].y = 0.0f;
pVertices[Current].z = 0.0f;
memset(&dPdU, 0, sizeof(D3DXVECTOR3));
memset(&dPdV, 0, sizeof(D3DXVECTOR3));
```

This nested loop sums the influences of each of the control points based on the values of the basis functions that were computed earlier.

```
for (long UStep = 0; UStep < 4; UStep++)
{
    for (long VStep = 0; VStep < 4; VStep++)
    {
```

First, compute the position of the vertex as the weighted sum of the influences of each control point. The control points are stored as 16 vertices at the beginning of the vertex buffer. This is essentially the code for Equation 7.1.

```
pVertices[Current].x += BU[UStep] * BV[VStep]
                * pVertices[UStep * 4 + VStep].x;
pVertices[Current].y += BU[UStep] * BV[VStep]
                * pVertices[UStep * 4 + VStep].y;
pVertices[Current].z += BU[UStep] * BV[VStep]
                * pVertices[UStep * 4 + VStep].z;
```

Likewise, the following lines are essentially the code for Equation 7.2. These will serve as the foundation for computing the normal vector.

```
dPdU.x += DU[UStep] * BV[VStep] *
            pVertices[UStep * 4 + VStep].x;
dPdU.y += DU[UStep] * BV[VStep] *
            pVertices[UStep * 4 + VStep].y;
dPdU.z += DU[UStep] * BV[VStep] *
            pVertices[UStep * 4 + VStep].z;

dPdV.x += BU[UStep] * DV[VStep] *
            pVertices[UStep * 4 + VStep].x;
dPdV.y += BU[UStep] * DV[VStep] *
            pVertices[UStep * 4 + VStep].y;
dPdV.z += BU[UStep] * DV[VStep] *
            pVertices[UStep * 4 + VStep].z;
    }
}
```

This is another bit of code that isn't entirely necessary. Here, I correct the vertex position down a little bit so that you can clearly see the control grid above the surface. If you don't care about seeing the grid, you can remove this line.

```
pVertices[Current].y -= 10.0f;
```

I begin computing the actual normal vector by normalizing the individual tangent vectors. This can be worthwhile because there are cases (such as bumpmapping) where you'd want the normalized tangent vectors in addition to the normal vector.

```
D3DXVec3Normalize(&dPdU, &dPdU);
D3DXVec3Normalize(&dPdV, &dPdV);
```

The cross product gives you the actual normal vector.

```
D3DXVec3Cross(&Normal, &dPdV, &dPdU);
```

Compute the lighting intensity as the dot product of the normal and the light direction. Keep in mind that the light direction vector was set as the opposite of the actual light direction.

```
float Intensity = D3DXVec3Dot(&Normal,
&LightDirection);
```

Clamp the intensity to 0. If the normal is facing away from the light, the intensity is 0. Once the value has been clamped, I set the vertex color to equal the intensity of the light. This assumes the light color is white. This is the last step for a given vertex.

```
if (Intensity < 0.0f) Intensity = 0.0f;

pVertices[Current].color =
D3DCOLOR_COLORVALUE(Intensity, Intensity, Inten
sity, 1.0f);
        }
    }
```

All vertices have been set. Unlock the buffer and return so the `Render` function can draw the surface.

```
        m_pPatchVertices->Unlock();
        return TRUE;
}
```

These pieces fit together to provide a general application framework plus the specific code needed to draw a Bezier surface. Figure 7.11 shows a screenshot from the application. Notice how the changes to both the x and y values create warping in two directions. The mesh is also correctly shaded as if a light was shining straight down.

Figure 7.12 shows the same mesh as a wireframe. Wireframes can be helpful in understanding exactly how the vertices move.

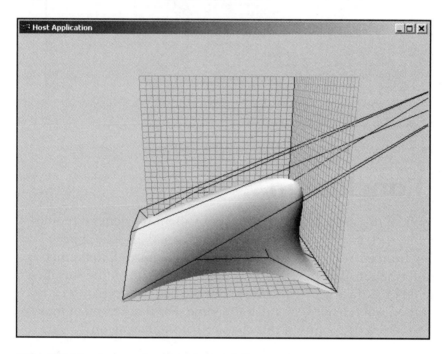

Figure 7.11   *A screenshot of the Bezier surface.*

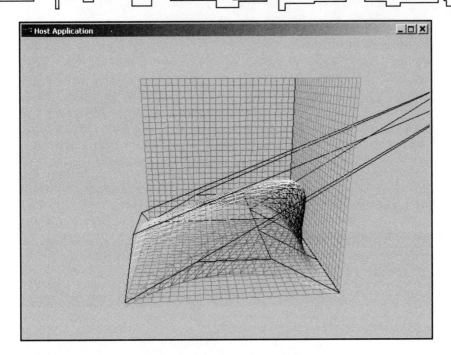

Figure 7.12 *A screenshot of the Bezier surface in wireframe.*

In Conclusion...

The bulk of this chapter was actually more about the general rendering framework than it was about Bezier surfaces. This is because moving from curves to surfaces really doesn't require all that much new information. The next chapters will concentrate on the specifics of the other surface representations, but the basic concepts and application will remain very much the same. For that reason, it makes sense to review the points of this chapter before moving on.

- Surfaces are built upon the same concepts as curves. The biggest difference is that the parametric space is now 2D.

- Like curves, the position on a surface is the weighted sum of the control points where the influence of each point is determined by the basis functions. For a surface, you use basis functions in both dimensions.

- The normal vector for any given point on the surface can be computed as the cross product of two vectors that are tangent to the surface at that point. Conveniently, you can use partial derivatives to get the tangents in the u and v directions.

- All of the samples use diffuse lighting, which is computed as the dot product of the normal vector and the opposite of the light direction.

- All of the surface applications use the same basic 3D framework.

- All of the surface applications use the same basic format for the vertex and index buffers.

CHAPTER 8

B-Spline Surfaces

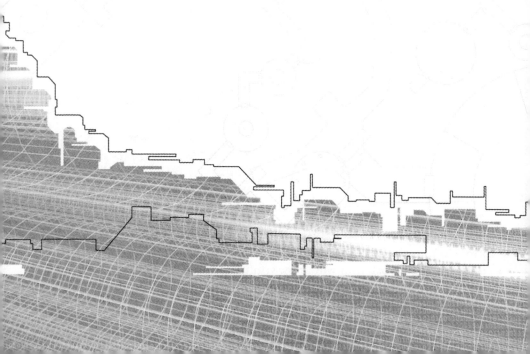

B ezier surfaces suffer from the same limitations present in Bezier curves. In this chapter, I will explain how to build surfaces based on B-spline concepts. Many of the basic ideas will carry over from Chapter 7, "Basic Surface Concepts and Bezier Surfaces," but I will introduce the following new material:

- Advantages of B-splines over Bezier surfaces
- Extending B-spline curves to surfaces
- Implementing B-spline surfaces

Advantages of B-Spline Surfaces over Bezier Surfaces

Chapter 7 presented Bezier patches as a simple way of introducing you to surfaces, but Bezier patches suffer from the same limitations as Bezier curves. For more complex shapes, you need to add more control points, but that raises the degree of the surface. You can join multiple surfaces together, but continuity considerations make that a nontrivial task. In the end, I omitted discussions about joining Bezier surfaces because you can achieve similar results more easily if you move to B-spline or NURBS surfaces.

The advantage of using B-spline surfaces is the same as the advantage you saw with B-spline curves. You can create a surface with many more control points without necessarily raising the degree of the surface. The surface in Chapter 7 was hardcoded to be a cubic surface defined by a 4x4 control grid. In this chapter, I introduce a

> **NOTE**
> Remember, if you really want to deal with Bezier surfaces, you can treat them as a special case of B-splines and render them using this flexible framework.

general framework that will allow you to use an arbitrary number of control points to create a surface of arbitrary order. Also, the surface can be of different order in the u and v directions. In the end, this is a much more flexible system than what you saw in Chapter 7.

In many ways, this chapter is a bridge between the basic concepts shown in Chapter 7 and the richer NURBS concepts in Chapter 9 and beyond. In this chapter, I will keep the basic application framework, but revamp the surface computations to the more flexible B-spline form that will serve as a foundation for the NURBS surfaces. Before I can talk about extending rational splines to surfaces, I need to talk about extending standard B-splines to surfaces.

From B-Spline Curves to Surfaces

In Chapter 7, you saw that Bezier curves and Bezier surfaces shared essentially the same equations. The only difference was that the surface equation employed basis functions in both parametric directions. B-spline surfaces are no different. Equation 8.1 extends B-spline curves to surfaces. In this case, k is the order in the u direction and l is the order in the v direction.

$$P(u,v) = \sum_{i=1}^{N} \sum_{j=1}^{M} P_{i,j} N_{i,k}(u) N_{j,l}(v)$$

Equation 8.1 *Equation for B-spline Surfaces.*

The basis functions are derived exactly as they were in Chapter 4, "B-Splines." For clarity, I repeat them in Equation 8.2, but they are the same as you saw in Equation 4.1.

This implies several things. First of all, the order can be different in both directions. Also, you can have different knot vectors in the two parametric directions. In all, the concepts you learned in Chapter 4 all apply here and can be applied differently in the u and v directions. For instance, the surface might be uniform and open in the u direction and periodic in the v direction. For a tube-shaped surface, you might want to use the techniques used to define a closed shape in one direction and use a simple second-order line in the other.

$$N_{i,1}(u) = \begin{cases} 1 \text{ if } x_i \le u < x_{i+1} \\ 0 \text{ otherwise} \end{cases}$$

$$N_{i,k}(u) = \frac{(u - x_i)N_{i,k-1}(u)}{x_{i+k-1} - x_i} + \frac{(x_{i+k} - u)N_{i+1,k-1}(u)}{x_{i+k} - x_{i+1}}$$

$$N_{j,1}(v) = \begin{cases} 1 \text{ if } y_j \le v < y_{j+1} \\ 0 \text{ otherwise} \end{cases}$$

$$N_{j,l}(v) = \frac{(v - y_j)N_{j,l-1}(v)}{y_{j+l-1} - y_j} + \frac{(y_{j+l} - v)N_{j+1,l-1}(v)}{y_{j+l} - y_{j+1}}$$

Equation 8.2 *B-spline surface basis functions.*

Computing the normal vector on a B-spline surface follows the same basic technique that was shown in Chapter 7. First, you need to express the partial derivatives of Equation 8.1 with respect to u and v as shown in Equation 8.3.

$$\frac{dP}{du} = \sum_{i=1}^{N} \sum_{j=1}^{M} P_{i,j} \frac{dN_{i,k}(u)}{du} N_{j,l}(v)$$

$$\frac{dP}{dv} = \sum_{i=1}^{N} \sum_{j=1}^{M} P_{i,j} N_{i,k}(u) \frac{dN_{j,l}(v)}{dv}$$

Equation 8.3 *Partial derivatives of Equation 8.1.*

Then, you need to find the derivatives of the basis functions (see Equation 8.4). The two derivatives are both instances of the derivatives you used in Chapter 4.

Once you have all the pieces, the normal vector itself is computed using the code shown in Chapter 7.

$$\frac{dN_{i,k}}{du} = \frac{N_{i,k-1}(u)+(u-x_i)\dfrac{dN_{i,k-1}}{du}}{x_{i+k-1}-x_i} +$$

$$\frac{(x_{i+k}-u)\dfrac{dN_{i+1,k-1}(u)}{du}-N_{i+1,k-1}(u)}{x_{i+k}-x_{i+1}}$$

$$\frac{dN_{j,l}}{dv} = \frac{N_{j,l-1}(v)+(v-y_i)\dfrac{dN_{j,l-1}}{dv}}{y_{j+l-1}-y_j} +$$

$$\frac{(y_{j+l}-v)\dfrac{dN_{j+1,l-1}(v)}{dv}-N_{j+1,l-1}(v)}{y_{j+l}-y_{j+1}}$$

Equation 8.4 *Derivatives of the basis functions.*

This is basically all you need in terms of theory. If you already understand B-spline curves, surfaces are actually very straightforward. If you still aren't sure how the 2D pieces fit together, the implementation will probably clarify things.

Implementing B-Spline Surfaces

The code for this chapter is on the CD in the \Code\Chapter08 - B-Spline Patches directory. As I said in Chapter 7, all of the real magic now happens in FillPatchBuffer. However, the magic requires a bit of setup. First, take a look at BSplinePatchApplication.h. There are now defined values for the order of both dimensions as well as the number of control points in each direction.

```
#define NUM_U_POINTS 5
#define NUM_V_POINTS 5

#define PATCH_ORDER_U   3
#define PATCH_ORDER_V   3
```

In this case, I have set the same number of points and the same order in both u and v, but that is not a requirement. I will use different values in later chapters, but you should also feel free to experiment. Just remember that the order should not exceed the number of control points.

A few lines down in the class definition, you will see that there are now two arrays for the knot vectors, two arrays for precomputed basis values, and two arrays of precomputed values for the derivatives.

```
float          m_KnotVectorU[NUM_U_POINTS + PATCH_ORDER_U];
float          m_KnotVectorV[NUM_V_POINTS + PATCH_ORDER_V];


float          m_BasisFunctionsU[NUM_PATCH_VERTICES]
                                 [NUM_U_POINTS][PATCH_ORDER_U];
float          m_DerivativeBasisU[NUM_PATCH_VERTICES]
                                 [NUM_U_POINTS][PATCH_ORDER_U];


float          m_BasisFunctionsV[NUM_PATCH_VERTICES]
                                 [NUM_V_POINTS][PATCH_ORDER_V];
float          m_DerivativeBasisV[NUM_PATCH_VERTICES]
                                 [NUM_V_POINTS][PATCH_ORDER_V];
```

Conceptually, these are the same arrays you saw in Chapter 4. There are now two sets because there are two parametric directions.

If you look at BSplinePatchApplication.cpp, you will see code for the setup functions SetKnotVectors and DefineBasisFunctions. I have not included the code here in the text because it is basically identical to the code you saw in Chapter 4. The only real difference is that SetKnotVectors now sets two different knot vectors and DefineBasisFunctions sets the values for both the u and v direction. This doubles the amount of code, but the computation is exactly the same as what you saw in Chapter 4.

Once everything is set up, the render loop calls FillPatchBuffer to actually compute the positions of the vertices before rendering. These vertices are rendered using the code outlined in Chapter 7.

```
BOOL CBSplinePatchApplication::FillPatchBuffer()
{
```

I have omitted the preliminary code that is an exact duplicate of the code shown in Chapter 7. The omitted code locks the vertex buffer, creates a uniform control grid, animates some of the control points, and creates the lighting variables. Once that has been done, the actual B-spline computation begins. As you saw in Chapter 7, the code loops and computes the position of each vertex for a given u and v value. The following code is the interior of that loop. Please see the code on the CD for the complete listing.

The loop defines a u and v value as U and V. First, you need to map that 2D value to the equivalent index in the 1D vertex buffer. Once you have that, the first order of business is to initialize all values to zero to facilitate summing the effects of the control points.

```
long Current = (NUM_U_POINTS * NUM_V_POINTS) + (U * NUM_PATCH_VERTICES)
+ V;

pVertices[Current].x = 0.0f;
pVertices[Current].y = 0.0f;
pVertices[Current].z = 0.0f;
memset(&dPdU, 0, sizeof(D3DXVECTOR3));
memset(&dPdV, 0, sizeof(D3DXVECTOR3));
```

The values of U and V are between 0 and NUM_PATCH_VERTICES. Here, I'm mapping them to values between 0 and 1. This will allow me to compare the current u and v values to the values in the knot vector. The knot vector determines the range of influence for each control point. I can optimize the calculations by ignoring the effects of control points that have no effect on this particular point. I will go into more detail about this below.

```
float CurrentU = (float)U / (float)(NUM_PATCH_VERTICES - 1);
float CurrentV = (float)V / (float)(NUM_PATCH_VERTICES - 1);
```

The following loops step through each control point in order to sum the influences.

```
for (long UStep = 0; UStep < NUM_U_POINTS; UStep++)
{
        for (long VStep = 0; VStep < NUM_V_POINTS; VStep++)
        {
```

This if statement is the key to the very simple (but potentially power-ful) optimization. It checks the knot vector values to see if the current (u, v) point is affected by the current (UStep, VStep) control point. If the current point falls outside of the range of influence, the control point is skipped entirely. This can save very many calculations in cases where the order of the surface is much lower than the number of control points.

```
if (m_KnotVectorU[UStep] <= CurrentU &&
    CurrentU <= m_KnotVectorU[UStep + PATCH_ORDER_U] &&
    m_KnotVectorV[VStep] <= CurrentV &&
    CurrentV <= m_KnotVectorV[VStep + PATCH_ORDER_V])
{
```

The vertex position is set using the 2D equivalent to the code you saw in Chapter 4. This is essentially the code for Equation 8.1.

```
pVertices[Current].x += pVertices[UStep *
                        NUM_V_POINTS + VStep].x *
                        m_BasisFunctionsU[U][UStep]
                        [PATCH_ORDER_U - 1] *
                        m_BasisFunctionsV[V][VStep]
                        [PATCH_ORDER_V - 1];
pVertices[Current].y += pVertices[UStep *
                        NUM_V_POINTS + VStep].y *
                        m_BasisFunctionsU[U][UStep]
                        [PATCH_ORDER_U - 1] *
                        m_BasisFunctionsV[V][VStep]
                        [PATCH_ORDER_V - 1];
pVertices[Current].z += pVertices[UStep *
                        NUM_V_POINTS + VStep].z *
                        m_BasisFunctionsU[U][UStep]
                        [PATCH_ORDER_U - 1] *
                        m_BasisFunctionsV[V][VStep]
                        [PATCH_ORDER_V - 1];
```

The tangent vectors are found using the 2D equivalent to the slope code you saw in Chapter 4. This is basically the same code as I showed in Chapter 7, only this time the B-spline derivatives are used in place of the Bezier derivatives.

```
      dPdU.x += pVertices[UStep * NUM_V_POINTS + VStep].x *
               m_DerivativeBasisU[U][UStep][PATCH_ORDER_U - 1] *
               m_BasisFunctionsV[V][VStep][PATCH_ORDER_V - 1];
      dPdU.y += pVertices[UStep * NUM_V_POINTS + VStep].y *
               m_DerivativeBasisU[U][UStep][PATCH_ORDER_U - 1] *
               m_BasisFunctionsV[V][VStep][PATCH_ORDER_V - 1];
      dPdU.z += pVertices[UStep * NUM_V_POINTS + VStep].z *
               m_DerivativeBasisU[U][UStep][PATCH_ORDER_U - 1] *
               m_BasisFunctionsV[V][VStep][PATCH_ORDER_V - 1];

      dPdV.x += pVertices[UStep * NUM_V_POINTS + VStep].x *
               m_BasisFunctionsU[U][UStep][PATCH_ORDER_U - 1] *
               m_DerivativeBasisV[V][VStep][PATCH_ORDER_V - 1];
      dPdV.y += pVertices[UStep * NUM_V_POINTS + VStep].y *
               m_BasisFunctionsU[U][UStep][PATCH_ORDER_U - 1] *
               m_DerivativeBasisV[V][VStep][PATCH_ORDER_V - 1];
      dPdV.z += pVertices[UStep * NUM_V_POINTS + VStep].z *
               m_BasisFunctionsU[U][UStep][PATCH_ORDER_U - 1] *
               m_DerivativeBasisV[V][VStep][PATCH_ORDER_V - 1];
    }
  }
}
```

After the position and tangents are computed, the normal vector is computed just as it was in Chapter 7, and the lighting value is set as the vertex color. Figure 8.1 shows a screenshot of the resulting surface.

In addition to showing the surface, Figure 8.1 also shows another feature of this application. I have added code that draws the basis functions for both u and v. I have not included the code here because it's very similar to the code shown in the curve chapters, but you can find it in the source code on the CD.

Figure 8.1 doesn't really demonstrate why B-spline surfaces are better than Bezier surfaces. Figure 8.2 shows another screenshot, only this time the number of control points in the u direction has been greatly increased.

The surface in Figure 8.2 has much more flexibility than most Bezier curves. Also, notice how the ranges shown on the basis function graphs correspond to the shape of the bulge in the surface. You could explicitly

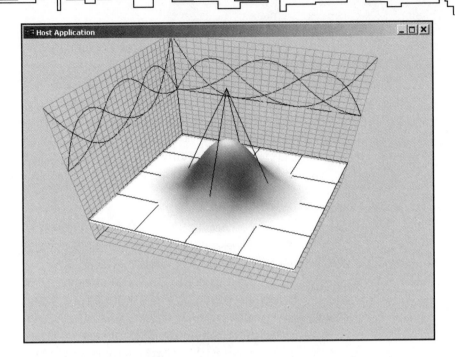

Figure 8.1 *A simple B-spline surface.*

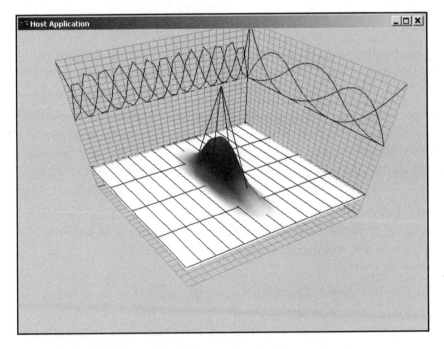

Figure 8.2 *A B-spline surface with more control points.*

set the values in the knot vector to control the way each of the control points affects the surface. Figure 8.3 shows the same surface, only this time the knot vector has been changed (as you can see from the graphs of the basis functions).

In the next chapter, you will see more examples of the level of control you can achieve with B-spline surfaces when I demonstrate different shapes with NURBS.

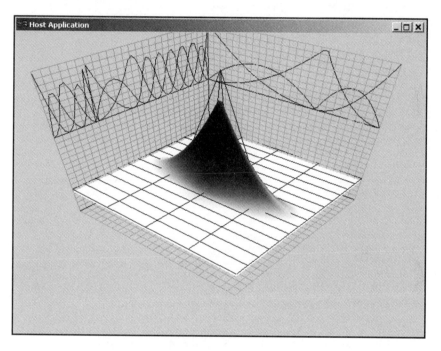

Figure 8.3 *A B-spline surface with nonuniform knot vectors.*

In Conclusion...

The relatively short length of this chapter is indicative of the fact that surfaces are relatively simple extensions of the concepts you should already know. In the next chapter, I will provide the same explanations for NURBS surfaces before moving on to different kinds of surfaces in Chapter 10, "More NURBS Surfaces." Before I get too far ahead of myself, let me review:

- B-spline surfaces are just extensions of B-spline curves into a second parametric dimension.

- The same advantages of B-spline curves apply to B-spline surfaces. You get more control over the shape and the degree of the surface.

- The u and v directions are each controlled by their own knot vectors and can be of different degrees.

- You can simplify the calculations if you use the knot vector to decide whether or not a given control point affects a given point on the surface.

CHAPTER 9

NURBS
SURFACES

This chapter completes the journey from Bezier surfaces to NURBS surfaces in much the same way that Chapters 3 through 5 moved from Bezier curves to NURBS curves. NURBS surfaces are the superset of all the previously described surfaces, which is why you see NURBS modeling tools and not B-spline modeling tools. The tendency among many developers is to use those tools for modeling, but then to export a polygonal mesh for the actual game. As you read this chapter, consider advantages of using NURBS in your game. In many cases, you'll have to create polygons before you actually render, but you can use the NURBS information to generate different levels of detail. Also, hardware support for higher-order surfaces is becoming more prevalent. In the future, you might not have to generate your own polygons.

By now, you know all of the basic ideas and you will see that NURBS surfaces are not all that different from the B-spline surfaces in Chapter 8. This chapter will cover the following material:

- Advantages of NURBS surfaces over B-spline surfaces
- Extending NURBS to two dimensions
- Implementing NURBS surfaces
- An example of a NURBS surface that is more useful than the "wavy sheet" examples in previous chapters
- A look at the size and bandwidth advantages of a NURBS model

Advantages of NURBS Surfaces over B-Spline Surfaces

To make a long story short, the advantages of NURBS surfaces over B-spline surfaces are essentially the same as the advantages described in the curve chapters. A NURBS representation gives you more control over the surface in the form of weights for the control points. NURBS surfaces are also better formulated for creating shapes from conic sections. In this chapter, I concentrate more on sheets in order to introduce the material, but Chapter 10, "More NURBS Surfaces," will provide examples of where the ability to model conic sections provides the basis for simple models of some fundamental shapes.

Of course, one other advantage is simply that NURBS represent a superset of B-spline surfaces. Therefore, if you are going to implement B-spline surfaces, you might as well implement them in the form of NURBS. A NURBS system may require more computational overhead, but that might not be an issue if your geometry is fairly static.

This chapter and the next will demonstrate some of the types of shapes that are possible with NURBS surfaces. The samples in Chapter 10 are heavily dependent on conic sections, which are only possible with NURBS. In some ways, the advantages of NURBS are implicit in the examples in Chapter 10. However, before I can talk about those examples, I need to explain some of the basics.

From NURBS Curves to Surfaces

By now you know the basics of applying your knowledge of curves to surfaces. You first extend the curve equations to two dimensions and then you compute partial derivatives that will be used to generate the tangent vectors. These tangent vectors are used to compute the surface normal vectors. As you can see in Equation 9.1, the equation for a NURBS surface is essentially the same as Equation 8.1 with the added weighting factor.

$$P(u,v) = \frac{\displaystyle\sum_{i=1}^{N}\sum_{j=1}^{M} W_{i,j} P_{i,j} N_{i,k}(u) N_{j,l}(v)}{\displaystyle\sum_{i=1}^{N}\sum_{j=1}^{M} W_{i,j} N_{i,k}(u) N_{j,l}(v)}$$

Equation 9.1 *Equation for NURBS Surfaces.*

Like B-spline surfaces, the knot vectors in the u and v directions are independent. There can be different knot values, different orders, and so on. However, the weight values are properties of the control points. Therefore, the weight for a particular point is the same in both the u and v directions. This is why you see two independent knot vectors but not two independent weight vectors. This is shown graphically in Figure 9.1. Each control point has a weight and there are independent sets of basis functions in the u and v directions.

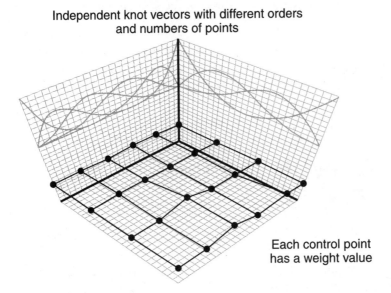

Independent knot vectors with different orders and numbers of points

Each control point has a weight value

Figure 9.1   *The building blocks of a NURBS surface.*

The partial derivatives of the equations in Equation 9.1 look quite intimidating, but they are derived using the same basic approaches outlined in Appendix A, "Derivative Calculus," and first seen in Chapter 7, " Basic Surface Concepts and Bezier Surfaces." Equation 9.2 shows the partial derivatives of Equation 9.1 with respect to u and v.

The equations are not nearly as frightening as they may seem. If you are uncomfortable with the equations, refer back to Appendix A and Chapter 5, "NURBS," and then apply the quotient rule to Equation 9.1. Writing out the equations should make them clearer. Also, the programmatic implementation should shed more light on how the numbers actually come together.

$$\frac{dP}{du} = P(u,v) \left(\frac{\displaystyle\sum_{i=1}^{N}\sum_{j=1}^{M} W_{i,j}P_{i,j}\frac{N_{i,k}(u)}{du}N_{j,l}(v)}{\displaystyle\sum_{i=1}^{N}\sum_{j=1}^{M} W_{i,j}P_{i,j}N_{i,k}(u)N_{j,l}(v)} - \frac{\displaystyle\sum_{i=1}^{N}\sum_{j=1}^{M} W_{i,j}\frac{N_{i,k}(u)}{du}N_{j,l}(v)}{\displaystyle\sum_{i=1}^{N}\sum_{j=1}^{M} W_{i,j}N_{i,k}(u)N_{j,l}(v)} \right)$$

$$\frac{dP}{dv} = P(u,v) \left(\frac{\displaystyle\sum_{i=1}^{N}\sum_{j=1}^{M} W_{i,j}P_{i,j}N_{i,k}(u)\frac{N_{j,l}(v)}{dv}}{\displaystyle\sum_{i=1}^{N}\sum_{j=1}^{M} W_{i,j}P_{i,j}N_{i,k}(u)N_{j,l}(v)} - \frac{\displaystyle\sum_{i=1}^{N}\sum_{j=1}^{M} W_{i,j}N_{i,k}(u)\frac{N_{j,l}(v)}{dv}}{\displaystyle\sum_{i=1}^{N}\sum_{j=1}^{M} W_{i,j}N_{i,k}(u)N_{j,l}(v)} \right)$$

Equation 9.2   *Partial derivatives of Equation 9.1.*

Implementing NURBS Surfaces

The code for this chapter is on the CD in the \Code\Chapter09 - NURBS Patches directory. The code is in many ways very similar to the code from Chapter 8. Therefore, I am only going to highlight the changes.

The first change is the inclusion of a 2D weight vector. The weight vector contains a weight value for each of the control points in the 2D control grid.

```
float   m_Weights[NUM_U_POINTS][NUM_V_POINTS];
```

The source code also includes a function that sets the weight values for each of these points. Currently, those values are set to 1.0 but feel free to experiment with different values. I chose not to highlight the effects of changing weights because the principles are the same as you saw in the curves chapters.

As you can see in Equations 9.1 and 9.2, the weight values are multiplied with different combinations of basis functions and their derivatives depending on the situation. Therefore, I do not include weight values when I precompute the basis functions. In fact, the code in

`DefineBasisFunctions` is exactly the same as in Chapter 8. In the previous chapters, I pointed out that all the magic happens in `FillPatchBuffer`. This is especially true in this chapter because there are more calculations that need to be done to incorporate the weight values. I will walk you through the code for `FillPatchBuffer` and you'll see that the bulk of the code is basically the NURBS equations in C++ form.

```
BOOL CNURBSPatchApplication::FillPatchBuffer()
{
```

For the sake of brevity, I have chosen to omit the first several lines that lock the vertex buffer and set the positions of the control points. See the code on the CD for the complete listing and feel free to change the control point positions to see the effects on the surface. The following code is focused on the actual computation of the points on the NURBS surface. There is a main loop that loops through each of the vertices and computes the values based on the precached basis values, the weight values, and the control point positions. The following code is taken from the inside of those nested loops.

In order to make the calculations more readable, I have divided the equations into numerators and denominators for both the position calculations and the derivative calculations. The code will compute each piece separately and then put them together at the end.

```
float NumeratorMultiplier = 0.0f;
float Denominator         = 0.0f;
float DenominatorDU       = 0.0f;
float DenominatorDV       = 0.0f;
```

Figure 9.2 demonstrates how each of the values map to components of Equations 9.1 and 9.2.

This loop is used to apply the influences of each control point to the current vertex.

```
for (long UStep = 0; UStep < NUM_U_POINTS; UStep++)
{
        for (long VStep = 0; VStep < NUM_V_POINTS; VStep++)
        {
```

This conditional statement ensures that the NURBS computations are only applied if this particular control point actually affects this particular vertex. The savings here are more substantial than in Chapter 8 because there are more calculations with NURBS.

$$P(u,v) = \frac{\displaystyle\sum_{i=1}^{N}\sum_{j=1}^{M} W_{i,j}\,P_{i,j}\,\boxed{N_{i,k}(u)N_{j,l}(v)}}{\boxed{\displaystyle\sum_{i=1}^{N}\sum_{j=1}^{M} W_{i,j}\,N_{i,k}(u)N_{j,l}(v)}}$$

Numerator Multiplier

Denominator (also used as denominator in derivatives below)

Numerator Multiplier variable is reused twice below

DenominatorDU and DenominatorDV are shown below.*

$$\frac{dP}{du} = P(u,v)\left(\frac{\displaystyle\sum_{i=1}^{N}\sum_{j=1}^{M}\boxed{W_{i,j}}P_{i,j}\,\boxed{\frac{N_{i,k}(u)}{du}}\,N_{j,l}(v)}{\displaystyle\sum_{i=1}^{N}\sum_{j=1}^{M} W_{i,j}P_{i,j}N_{i,k}(u)N_{j,l}(v)} - \frac{\boxed{\displaystyle\sum_{i=1}^{N}\sum_{j=1}^{M} W_{i,j}\frac{N_{i,k}(u)}{du}N_{j,l}(v)}}{\displaystyle\sum_{i=1}^{N}\sum_{j=1}^{M} W_{i,j}N_{i,k}(u)N_{j,l}(v)}\right)$$

$$\frac{dP}{dv} = P(u,v)\left(\frac{\displaystyle\sum_{i=1}^{N}\sum_{j=1}^{M}\boxed{W_{i,j}}P_{i,j}\,\boxed{N_{i,k}(u)\frac{N_{j,l}(v)}{dv}}}{\displaystyle\sum_{i=1}^{N}\sum_{j=1}^{M} W_{i,j}P_{i,j}N_{i,k}(u)N_{j,l}(v)} - \frac{\boxed{\displaystyle\sum_{i=1}^{N}\sum_{j=1}^{M} W_{i,j}N_{i,k}(u)\frac{N_{j,l}(v)}{dv}}}{\displaystyle\sum_{i=1}^{N}\sum_{j=1}^{M} W_{i,j}N_{i,k}(u)N_{j,l}(v)}\right)$$

* Note: Don't be confused by the fact that DenominatorDU and DenominatorDV appear in the numerators of the equations above. These variables are the derivatives of the denominator with respect to u and v and the quotient rule yields the above equations.

Figure 9.2 *Mapping equations to variables.*

```
if (m_KnotVectorU[UStep] <= CurrentU &&
    CurrentU <= m_KnotVectorU[UStep + PATCH_ORDER_U] &&
    m_KnotVectorV[VStep] <= CurrentV &&
    CurrentV <= m_KnotVectorV[VStep + PATCH_ORDER_V])
{
```

This first denominator value is the denominator of Equation 9.1. Here I am summing the products of the weight of the control points and their "influence" as determined by the precomputed basis function values.

```
Denominator += m_Weights[UStep][VStep] *
        m_BasisFunctionsU[U][UStep][PATCH_ORDER_U - 1] *
        m_BasisFunctionsV[V][VStep][PATCH_ORDER_V - 1];
```

This second denominator value is the denominator of the partial derivative with respect to u, as shown in Figure 9.2.

```
DenominatorDU += m_Weights[UStep][VStep] *
        m_DerivativeBasisU[U][UStep][PATCH_ORDER_U - 1] *
        m_BasisFunctionsV[V][VStep][PATCH_ORDER_V - 1];
```

The final denominator value is the denominator of the partial derivative with respect to v. The three denominators are not actually used until after all the control points have been accounted for.

```
DenominatorDV += m_Weights[UStep][VStep] *
        m_BasisFunctionsU[U][UStep][PATCH_ORDER_U - 1] *
        m_DerivativeBasisV[V][VStep][PATCH_ORDER_V - 1];
```

The numerator multiplier variable is actually reused to compute several different numerators. First, I compute the numerator for Equation 9.1.

```
NumeratorMultiplier = m_Weights[UStep][VStep] *
        m_BasisFunctionsU[U][UStep][PATCH_ORDER_U - 1] *
        m_BasisFunctionsV[V][VStep][PATCH_ORDER_V - 1];
```

The control index is the index of this particular control point.

```
long ControlIndex = UStep * NUM_V_POINTS + VStep;
```

The position calculation is partially based on the product of the numerator multiplier value and the position of the control point. The following code is not the complete position calculation (you still need to divide by the denominator), but you can conveniently store the interim value in the vertex.

```
pVertices[Current].x += NumeratorMultiplier *
                        pVertices[ControlIndex].x;
pVertices[Current].y += NumeratorMultiplier *
                        pVertices[ControlIndex].y;
pVertices[Current].z += NumeratorMultiplier *
                        pVertices[ControlIndex].z;
```

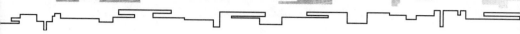

Now the numerator multiplier is used to store the scaling factor of the partial derivative with respect to u. This scales the effect of this control point on the tangent in the u direction.

```
NumeratorMultiplier = m_Weights[UStep][VStep] *
        m_DerivativeBasisU[U][UStep][PATCH_ORDER_U - 1] *
        m_BasisFunctionsV[V][VStep][PATCH_ORDER_V - 1];

dPdU.x += NumeratorMultiplier*
pVertices[ControlIndex].x;
dPdU.y += NumeratorMultiplier*
pVertices[ControlIndex].y;
dPdU.z += NumeratorMultiplier*
pVertices[ControlIndex].z;
```

Finally, the numerator multiplier is used to scale the effect of this control point on the tangent in the v direction.

```
NumeratorMultiplier= m_Weights[UStep][VStep] *
        m_BasisFunctionsU[U][UStep][PATCH_ORDER_U - 1] *
        m_DerivativeBasisV[V][VStep][PATCH_ORDER_V - 1];

dPdV.x += NumeratorMultiplier*
pVertices[ControlIndex].x;
dPdV.y += NumeratorMultiplier*
pVertices[ControlIndex].y;
dPdV.z += NumeratorMultiplier*
pVertices[ControlIndex].z;
                }
            }
        }
```

At this point, the code has looped through all of the control points and summed the influences into several intermediate variables. The following code brings all the factors together to generate the tangent vectors and the vertex position. The code completes the computations described by Equation 9.2.

```
dPdU.x = ((dPdU.x / Denominator) - (pVertices[Current].x *
        DenominatorDU / (Denominator * Denominator)));
```

```
dPdV.x = ((dPdV.x / Denominator) - (pVertices[Current].x *
         DenominatorDV / (Denominator * Denominator)));

dPdU.y = ((dPdU.y / Denominator) - (pVertices[Current].y *
         DenominatorDU / (Denominator * Denominator)));
dPdV.y = ((dPdV.y / Denominator) - (pVertices[Current].y *
         DenominatorDV / (Denominator * Denominator)));

dPdU.z = ((dPdU.z / Denominator) - (pVertices[Current].z *
         DenominatorDU / (Denominator * Denominator)));
dPdV.z = ((dPdV.z / Denominator) - (pVertices[Current].z *
         DenominatorDV / (Denominator * Denominator)));
```

The vertex already contains the results of all of the numerator calculations. The following lines factor in the denominator to complete the calculations shown in Equation 9.1.

```
pVertices[Current].x /= Denominator;
pVertices[Current].y /= Denominator;
pVertices[Current].z /= Denominator;
```

At this point, the calculations for position and tangent vectors are complete. The remainder of the loop applies the lighting calculations to compute the vertex color before moving on to the next vertex.

Figure 9.3 shows a screenshot of the application in action.

This particular patch could have been modeled with a B-spline patch, but I wanted to keep things very simple. Feel free to experiment with the weighting values to create different shapes and effects.

Moving Beyond Fluttering Sheets

So far, all of the surface examples have taken the form of sheets that are stretched and deformed as the control points change. This is an easy way to demonstrate the basics; not all that many game objects can be represented as rubber sheets. As a more real-world example, I have created the shape of a space ship, as shown in Figure 9.4.

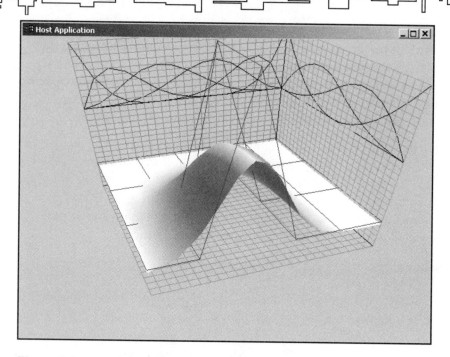

Figure 9.3 *Screenshot of a simple NURBS patch.*

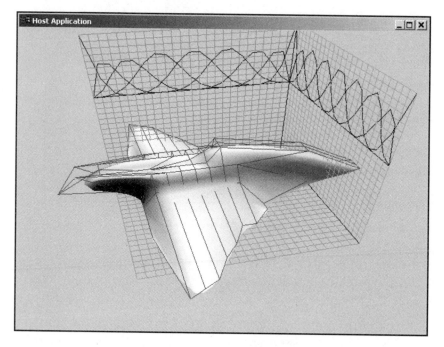

Figure 9.4 *NURBS space ship.*

The model is not complete (there is no bottom), but it still demonstrates all of the important points. First, it's important to note that the code is exactly the same as described earlier. The only things that have changed are the positions of the control points. The code can be found on the CD under Code\Chapter09 – NURBS Patch Model, and you can find the control point positions in the FillPatchBuffer function.

Notice that the model is no longer a wavy square shape. This is because the control points are no longer arranged in a square shape. Instead, the control points along the edge are shaped into the rough outline of the ship. Figures 9.5 and 9.6 demonstrate this. First, I started with a nonuniform grid of control points. This will allow me to put more detail and control in certain areas than in others.

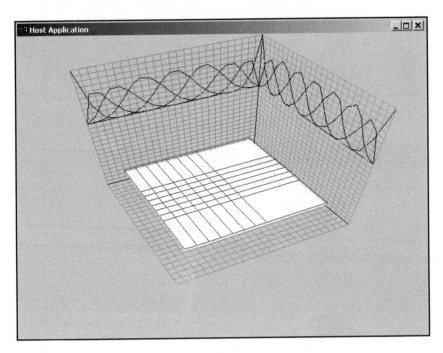

Figure 9.5 *Basic NURBS patch with nonuniform control grid.*

Next, the control points are moved to create the rough shape of the ship. I have disabled the height changes in this screenshot in order to emphasize the irregular shape.

Finally, the control point heights are changed to complete the ship. Figure 9.7 is basically the same shot as Figure 9.4, only now the model is drawn in wireframe so that you can see how the mesh is laid out.

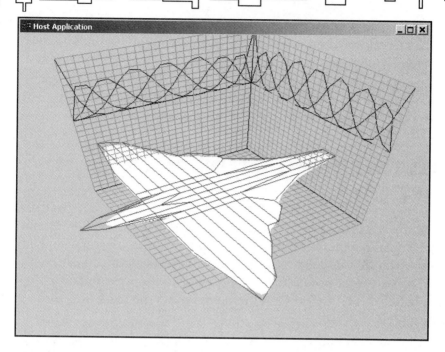

Figure 9.6   *Basic space ship shape.*

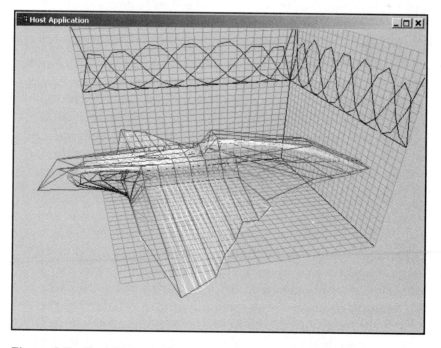

Figure 9.7   *Final ship in wireframe.*

The final object is much closer to something you'd actually use in a game. In a real-world situation, you probably wouldn't want to model the shape by hardcoding control point positions. Instead, you might want to create your own NURBS model format or use a NURBS modeler such as Rhino. However you choose to create the model, the NURBS representation does have some advantages.

Advantages of NURBS Surfaces

One of the advantages of a NURBS model over a traditional polygonal model is that mathematical formats are inherently more compact. For instance, you can model a circle as a set of N vertices, or you can model it as a center position and radius. The latter representation is much better if you want to send the model over a network or create various levels of detail.

A NURBS model is conceptually the same as the circle example. Figure 9.5 shows that 81 control points were used to generate the space ship model. In Figure 9.4, the model was rendered with 400 vertices. Including knot and weight vectors, the NURBS representation would still require roughly 75% less bandwidth to send over the network.

With the advent of DVDs and broadband, one could argue that bandwidth considerations are not as critical as they once were. That might or might not be true, but there is another advantage to NURBS. A mathematical representation is not tied to any one level of detail. This means that several equivalent models can be generated from the same control grid. Figure 9.8 shows three examples of the ship at different levels of detail. At the higher levels of detail, note the differences in the tail and where the wing meets the fuselage.

There are two points to be made here. The first is that now the same 81 control points can be used to represent many more vertices across more than one instantiation of the model. The other point is that one can imagine a system that tunes the model based on the end user's configuration. You can begin to imagine scenarios where the users upgrade their machine and your game not only runs faster, but the models actually "upgrade" themselves to be smoother. The control grid is far more compact and flexible than including a large number

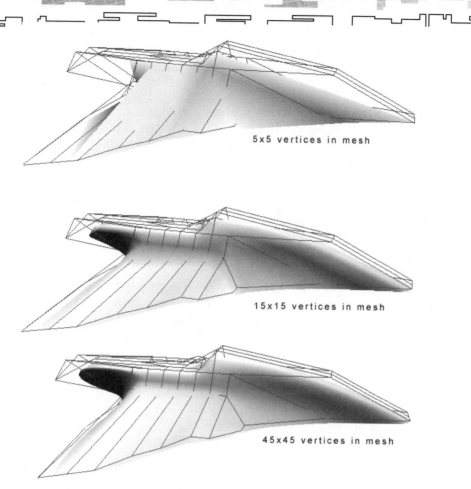

5x5 vertices in mesh

15x15 vertices in mesh

45x45 vertices in mesh

Figure 9.8 *Ships for yesterday, today, and tomorrow.*

of models on your DVD. Remember, the three models in Figure 9.8 are all based on the same NURBS representation.

One could argue that the same advantages could be achieved with subdivision surfaces and/or some of the hardware-based subdivision features. That might be true in some instances, but it might still be worthwhile to generate your own scalable meshes. In some instances, hardware subdivision is inappropriate because you need to know where the vertices are for computations such as collision detection or shadow generation.

There may also be occasions where you might want to use different levels of detail for different tasks. For example, you might generate a low-res model for collision detection, but a very high-res model for rendering. The results of the collision detection calculations could drive deformations of the control mesh that could then propagate to the high-res model.

It's an exciting time in computer graphics and there are many tools available to you. Different circumstances call for different solutions. It's important to understand the advantages of each solution and use whichever one makes the most sense.

In Conclusion...

This chapter completes the progression from simple Bezier surfaces to more flexible NURBS surfaces. The samples included with this chapter don't specifically take advantage of NURBS features, but all the groundwork is laid for you to experiment with changes to knot vectors, weights, and control point positions. I would recommend continuing on to the next chapter to see other examples. After that, you might want to return to this chapter to experiment with shapes and models of your own. Remember, it's okay to hack through the source code because you can always get a fresh copy off the CD if you make mistakes. Before moving into the samples in the next chapter, here's a quick review of the basic ideas.

- The NURBS equations are based on the same principles described in Chapter 5 and in Chapter 7. If you are uncomfortable with the equations, review those two chapters. Chapter 5 will refresh you on NURBS, and Chapter 7 describes the basics of moving to a 2D parametric space.

- The code for NURBS surfaces is extremely similar to the code for B-spline surfaces because I cache the basis function values in exactly the same way. The weight factors are not taken into account until `FillPatchBuffer` because of the way they factor into the partial derivatives.

- As usual, there are many areas of the code that could be optimized depending on how you wanted to optimize (memory vs. speed, and so on).

- The space ship example is used to show that NURBS surfaces are not just wavy sheets, but the same principles apply to B-spline surfaces as well. You could even implement the space ship as a Bezier surface, but you'd be subject to all the limitations of Bezier surfaces.

- The space ship was modeled by hardcoding vertex positions. There are NURBS tools such as Rhino that are much better for modeling.

- NURBS surfaces (or any of the other mathematical representations) have advantages over polygonal models because they encode the features of the surface in a more compact and flexible form.

CHAPTER 10

MORE
NURBS
SURFACES

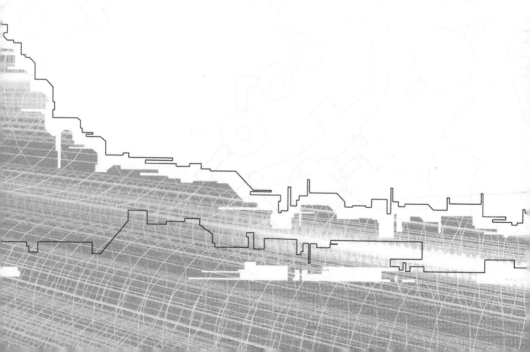

T he previous chapter covered the basic mathematics of NURBS surfaces and reinforced the fact that NURBS surfaces were not limited to rubber sheets. In this chapter, I'll take that notion further by introducing several techniques for modeling basic primitives. Unless noted otherwise, the math and basic application framework are exactly the same as the previous chapter. There are several sample projects for this chapter on the CD. In some cases, I'll refer to the source code, but in most cases the concepts are most easily explained with screenshots of the sample applications. I will cover the following new surface representations:

- Ruled surfaces
- Surfaces of revolution
- Swept surfaces
- Skinned surfaces

Ruled Surfaces

Ruled surfaces are very straightforward and do not require many changes to the sheets that you've seen in previous chapters. The idea is that you have a set of two or more shape curves in one parametric direction and you linearly interpolate between them in the other parametric direction. This is one of the basic tools that product, automobile, and ship designers use. If you know a set of profile shapes that roughly define a larger shape, you can use a ruled surface to interpolate between the profiles. From Chapter 3, "Parametric Equations and Bezier Curves," you know that you could describe a ruled surface between two curves with the following equation.

$$P(u,v) = (1-v)P(u,0) + vP(u,1)$$

Equation 10.1   *Equation for a basic ruled surface.*

One example of a ruled surface is shown in Figure 10.1. The surface in the screenshot is similar to a hanging curtain. One edge is straight and the other edge is a wavy shape. Each point between the two edges is linearly interpolated from those two shapes.

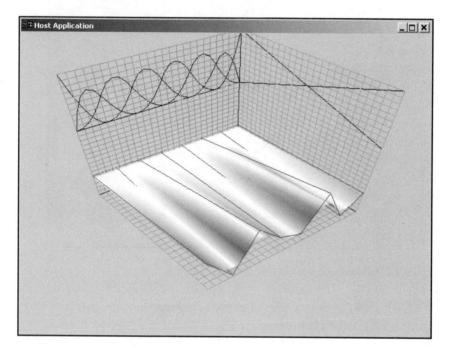

Figure 10.1 *A simple ruled surface.*

Take a look at the basis functions in the preceding figure. The shape curves have a higher order in the u direction, but the curve in the v direction is simply a second-order (linear) function. You could increase the number of shape curves by increasing the number of points in the v direction but staying with a second-order function. This is shown in Figure 10.2.

As you can see, you can implement ruled surfaces in the same basic NURBS framework used in Chapter 9. There are cases where this might not be true. For instance, the basic NURBS code does not include the ability to have two shape curves with different knot vectors. In that case, you would need to add more code, but the implementation would still be very straightforward.

Even if you keep the underlying framework as is, you might still want to provide a more intuitive interface to ruled surfaces. My framework

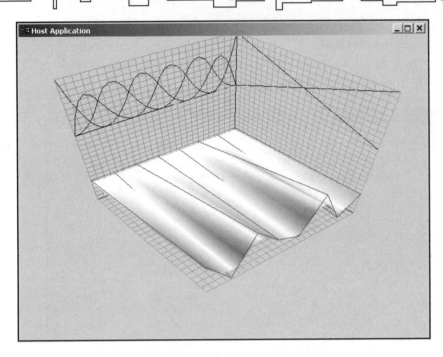

Figure 10.2   *A ruled surface with three shape curves.*

treats NURBS surfaces as a grid of control points. A more intuitive way of setting the control points might be to provide a function that accepts an array of profile curves. At a lower level, these profiles could be mapped to points in the grid.

Surfaces of Revolution

Another basic type of surface is a surface of revolution. The idea here is that you take one profile shape and rotate it around some axis of revolution. In manufacturing, this is the job of a *lathe*. A lathe is a machine that spins a piece of material and uses a cutting tool to cut the shape of the object as it spins. In most cases, the object is symmetric about the axis of revolution by virtue of the fact that the cutting tool cuts equally along the entire circumference as the object spins. Examples of such products are chair legs, candlesticks, and baseball bats.

One method for creating such a surface is to take a profile shape and interpolate over a circle using basic trigonometry. This is the most straightforward way, but you can use NURBS to do it in a much more flexible and elegant way. I'll explain the technique and then talk about why it is more flexible.

In Chapter 5, "NURBS," you learned that you could shape a NURBS curve into a circle with the appropriate control polygon and weight values. You can use the same basic approach to roll a NURBS surface into a cylinder. Simply adjust each of the control points to form circles in a given direction. Figure 10.3 shows two examples of cylinders "rolled" in the u direction.

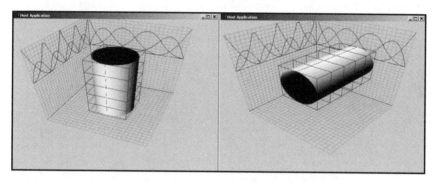

Figure 10.3 *NURBS cylinders.*

The cylinder is the most basic surface of revolution. In the case of a cylinder, the profile curve is a straight line at a constant distance from the center. Before moving to more interesting shapes, I'd like to point out one more important feature of Figure 10.3. In the previous chapters, the control points were located such that the uv parametric plane was the same as the xz plane. This might have contributed to the false impression that the two planes were related. This is not the case. The two cylinders in Figure 10.3 are both exactly the same in regard to u and v. The only difference is that the layout of the control points changes the axis of the cylinder. To put it a different way, the control points determine the relationship between the uv parametric space and the visual xyz space.

If you think of each row of control points in the u direction as a distinct control polygon, you can see that all points on the surface of the cylinder are equidistant from the center axis because all of the individual control polygons form circles of equal radii. You can create more interesting shapes by adjusting the radii of each of these circles. The order and knot vector of the surface in the v direction will determine how these circles are interpolated over the length of the axis. Figure 10.4 shows one example of a more interesting shape.

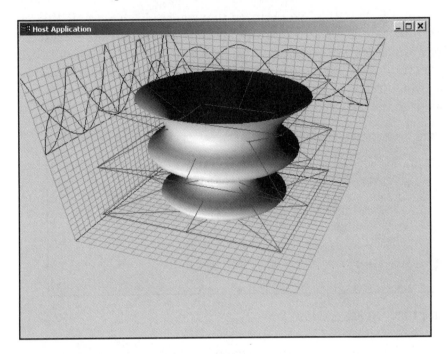

Figure 10.4 *A NURBS surface of revolution.*

One could argue that this shape could have been created much more simply. You could have created the profile shape and rotated the shape about some axis. That's true, but remember that these shapes are very useful as starting points. The NURBS representation gives you far more flexibility to make the shape more interesting.

For instance, you might model a rocket by starting with a cylinder. The result would be a symmetric shape similar to the one shown in Figure 10.3. You might then decide to pull individual control points to create fins for the rocket. The resulting shape would be similar to the one shown in Figure 10.5.

At this point, the shape is no longer technically a surface of revolution because it is no longer symmetric about its axis. This is not very important. What is important is that you were able to start with a basic, well-understood shape and quickly build interesting features onto it. You could not easily produce the shape in Figure 10.5 if you had started by simply rotating a profile curve around the axis.

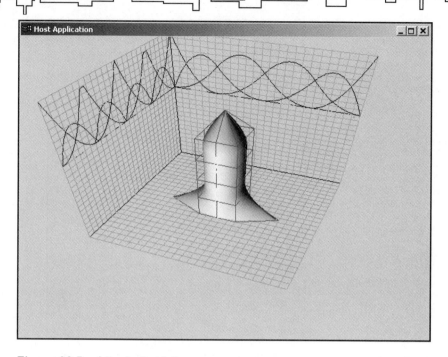

Figure 10.5   *A "rocket" with fins.*

Before moving on, I'd like to point out that a sphere can be modeled as a special case of a surface of revolution. In the case of a sphere, the profile curve is a semicircle. When the semicircle is rotated around a circular axis, the result is a sphere. Modeling a sphere with polygons is relatively straightforward, but the NURBS method would be better if you wanted to shape the model further. Once you start with a sphere, it would be very easy to model a teardrop or similar shapes. You could also animate the control points to easily "unwrap" the sphere.

Swept Surfaces

Swept surfaces could also be called extruded surfaces or loft surfaces. A swept surface is created when you sweep a shape along a path. Unlike a surface of revolution, the cross-section of a swept surface remains constant as you sweep along the path. This is analogous to pasta or any other material that is extruded with a constant cross-section. Figures 10.6 and 10.7 show how a shape and cross-section result in a swept surface.

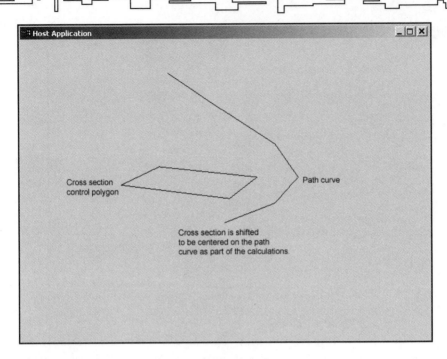

Figure 10.6   *The path and cross-section of a swept surface.*

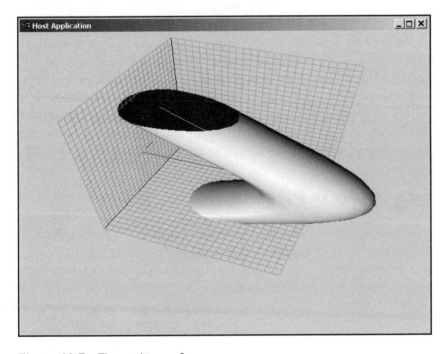

Figure 10.7   *The resulting surface.*

Mathematically, these surfaces are exactly the same as every NURBS surface you've seen, but I've set up the control net differently. Instead of a 2D grid of control points, swept surfaces are defined by two distinct curves. One curve is the cross section and the other is the path, as shown in Figure 10.6.

NOTE

I just finished making the point that the general **NURBS** patch was more flexible than a specialized representation. Now, I am introducing a special representation. Once I explain the basic idea, I will address this inconsistency and tell you how to formulate a more general approach.

In this example, I have set up the control points such that the cross section is defined by the u parameter and the path is defined by v. The vertex is also set up differently. The number of control points is now the sum of the u and v points instead of the product.

```
#define NUM_TOTAL_VERTICES (NUM_U_POINTS + NUM_V_POINTS +
                            NUM_PATCH_VERTICES * NUM_PATCH_VERTICES)
```

FillPatchBuffer also operates differently. For each value of u and v, the code now finds the position of each vertex as defined by the cross section shape and then adds that to the position as defined by the path. The fact that the cross section is always the same, allows you to rearrange calculations to be more efficient. Look at the source code for Chapter10, Swept Surfaces, to see how I rearranged the code. Other optimizations are available, but I kept changes minimal. The following is a small snippet of the code.

```
pVertices[Current].x += (NumeratorU * pVertices[ControlIndexU].x /
DenominatorU)
                        + (NumeratorV * pVertices[ControlIndexV].x /
                          DenominatorV);
pVertices[Current].y += (NumeratorU * pVertices[ControlIndexU].y /
DenominatorU)
                        + (NumeratorV * pVertices[ControlIndexV].y /
                          DenominatorV);
pVertices[Current].z += (NumeratorU * pVertices[ControlIndexU].z /
DenominatorU)
                        + (NumeratorV * pVertices[ControlIndexV].z /
                          DenominatorV);
```

In effect, this is shifting the cross section shape along the path curve. Figure 10.7 shows a simple cylinder. The cross section curve is the same at every point along the path, but it is shifted upward along the path. If the path were bent, the circular cross section would also be moved horizontally as shown in Figure 10.8.

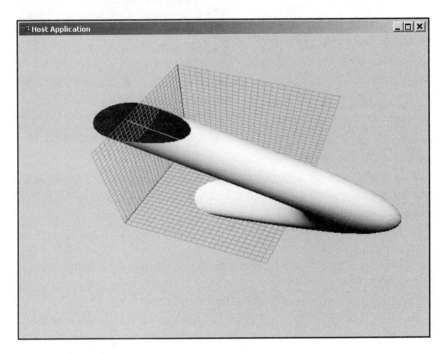

Figure 10.8   *Swept surface along a curved path.*

Figure 10.8 reveals a potential weakness of a swept surface. If the path is bent, you might want the shape to be bent as well. In that case, you really want a skinned surface.

Skinned Surfaces

A skinned surface is very similar to a swept surface. The difference is that the skinned surface correctly accounts for bends in the path curve. Figure 10.9 features the same path and cross section shown in Figure 10.8, only now the resulting surface is a skinned surface.

The basic code for the skinned surface is identical to swept surfaces in terms of how the NURBS calculations are carried out. The differences

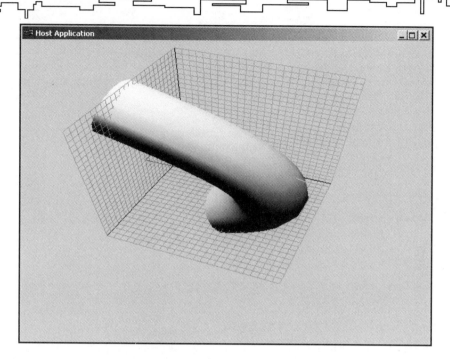

Figure 10.9 *Skinned surface instead of a swept surface.*

occur after all the NURBS calculations. The skinning portion involves a fair amount of vector calculations.

To understand the calculations, first consider the cross section curve. In the samples, the curve is constructed on the xz plane. This is not a requirement, but it does make things a little easier to visualize. You could define the cross section with whatever orientation you want (by moving the control points). The math will work out the same as long as you are consistent. If you think of the shape as lying on a plane, you can think of a normal vector to that plane as shown in Figure 10.10.

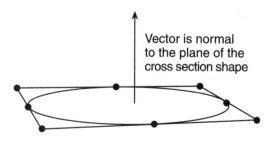

Vector is normal
to the plane of the
cross section shape

Figure 10.10 *Cross section and normal vector.*

As the path bends, you want the cross section to rotate accordingly. In effect, you want the normal of the cross section to match the tangent of the path curve, as shown in Figure 10.11.

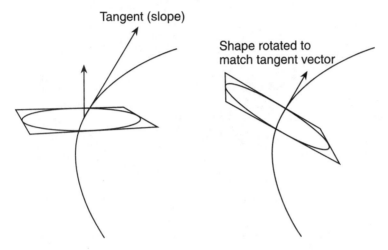

Tangent (slope)

Shape rotated to match tangent vector

Figure 10.11 *Rotating the cross section to match the tangent to the path.*

So, you have two vectors and you want to rotate one to match the other. This can be done fairly easily with the dot product and cross product. The cross product of any two vectors produces a third vector that is perpendicular to both. This will serve as an axis of rotation. In Figure 10.11, the axis is either into or out of the page (depending on how you order the cross product). If you rotate the cross section normal vector around that axis, you will eventually match the tangent vector.

The angle of the rotation is given by the dot product. The dot product of two normalized vectors yields the cosine of the angle between those vectors. The arccosine gives you the angle value. Once you know the angle and the axis, you can rotate the cross section to match the tangent. Figure 10.12 shows how all the steps fit together.

The code for this is straightforward. You have most of the pieces already. First, there is one difference in the position calculations. Instead of adding the u and v components together, the cross section shape is computed along with an offset value as shown next.

```
pVertices[Current].x += (NumeratorU * pVertices[ControlIndexU].x /
                         DenominatorU);
```

Rotate A around C axis to match B

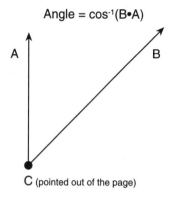

Angle = cos⁻¹(B•A)

$\text{Angle} = \cos^{-1}(B \bullet A)$

A

B

C (pointed out of the page)

C = B x A

Figure 10.12 *Rotating one vector to match another.*

```
VOffset.x += (NumeratorV * pVertices[ControlIndexV].x / DenominatorV);

pVertices[Current].y += (NumeratorU * pVertices[ControlIndexU].y /
                         DenominatorU);
VOffset.y += (NumeratorV * pVertices[ControlIndexV].y / DenominatorV);

pVertices[Current].z += (NumeratorU * pVertices[ControlIndexU].z /
                         DenominatorU);
VOffset.z += (NumeratorV * pVertices[ControlIndexV].z / DenominatorV);
```

The tangent vector for the path is dP/dV—the slope value that I have been calculating all along. Between the offset value and the tangent vector, you have everything you need to "skin" the surface. First, create a translation matrix. This will offset the cross section as you saw with swept surfaces. The reason for the matrix is that matrix transformations are order dependent. You need to offset the cross section after you rotate it.

```
D3DXMATRIX Translation;
D3DXMatrixTranslation(&Translation, VOffset.x, VOffset.y, VOffset.z);
```

I define a rotation matrix, an axis vector, and a base direction. The base direction is the normal vector of the cross section and I chose these values based on the fact that my shape is defined on the xz plane. If you choose to define the cross section differently, you will need to change the values. Also, note that both the base direction vector and the dPdV vector are normalized at this point.

```
D3DXMATRIX  Rotation;
D3DXVECTOR3 Axis;
D3DXVECTOR3 BaseDirection(0.0f, 1.0f, 0.0f);
```

The angle value is the arccosine of the dot product of the two vectors. The axis of rotation is given by the cross product.

```
float Angle = acos(D3DXVec3Dot(&BaseDirection, &dPdV));
D3DXVec3Cross(&Axis, &BaseDirection, &dPdV);
```

The D3DX library provides a convenient function to create a rotation matrix from an angle and an axis of rotation. This gives you the rotation matrix:

```
D3DXMatrixRotationAxis(&Rotation, &Axis, Angle);
```

The D3DX library also provides an easy way to transform a point with a matrix. Here, I concatenate the translation and rotation matrices and use them to transform the vertex position.

```
D3DXVec3TransformCoord((D3DXVECTOR3 *)&(pVertices[Current]),
                       (D3DXVECTOR3 *)&(pVertices[Current]),
                       &(Rotation * Translation));
```

The result is a vertex on a skinned surface as shown in Figure 10.9. These simple bent cylinders are starting to look as boring as the rubber sheet examples, so I also provided a sample that uses skinned surfaces to model a spring, as shown in Figure 10.13.

The code for the spring is also on the CD. Basically, I defined a helical path shape and a circular cross section. After that, the code is exactly the same as any other skinned surface. This can be interesting because you can begin to think about higher-level parametric shapes. For instance, you could easily write a function that produces any type of spring based on a diameter, a height, number of turns, and level of detail. The resulting mesh can be easily generated with the now familiar NURBS calculations.

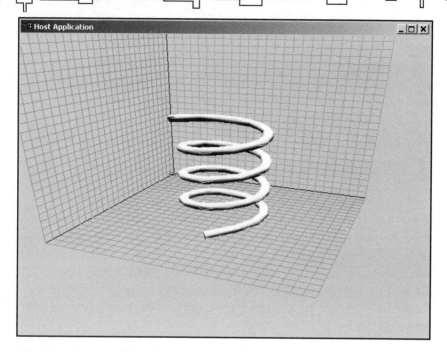

Figure 10.13 *A skinned spring.*

Generalizing Swept and Skinned Shapes

I made a point of modeling surfaces of revolution as a control net for the sake of flexibility. Then, I turned around and introduced custom code for swept and skinned surfaces. These forms are not as flexible. For instance, you might want to transform the spring into a snake by expanding the end into a head and perhaps produce a rattle on the tail. This is not easy with the current form.

If you want to create a more flexible shape, you can do so by defining a surface with three different parametric curves. In this case, u and v would be the surface as you saw with surfaces of revolution and a new w curve could be the path shape. You could model the shape by combining the pieces you already have. First, use the skinning/sweeping code to position uv control points along the w path instead of vertices. Then, use the uv calculations to create the actual vertices. This might sound complex, but you have all the basic pieces at your fingertips.

Remember that such a representation can be heavier than the simple path and cross section method. The spring, for example, would require many more control points if modeled this way. For simple skinned or swept shapes, the code provided on the CD will be quite adequate. However, if you feel comfortable with the material, you might want to implement the other method as an exercise.

In Conclusion...

By now, you have seen how the NURBS equations can be used to create a wide variety of surfaces. The examples in this chapter serve to introduce several different classes of surfaces that can serve as starting points. In most cases, that's all they are. For instance, you might model a character's head by starting with a surface of revolution, creating a sphere, and then manipulating individual control points to create the facial features. The application might be quite different, but the math is exactly the same.

This chapter concludes all the NURBS material. You now have several tools available to you. At this point, I'd recommend taking some time to experiment with different shapes and trying to solidify your understanding of how everything works. Here are some important things to remember from this chapter.

- Ruled surfaces are created when you interpolate between two or more shape curves. This can be done in the context of the basic NURBS framework or you could reformulate the code to specifically deal with ruled surfaces.

- Surfaces of revolution are created when you rotate a profile shape about an axis. The result is a shape that is symmetric about the axis of rotation with a varying cross section.

- Swept surfaces are created when you sweep a shape curve along a path curve. This allows you to create shapes that are not symmetric about an axis, but have a constant cross section.

- The potential downside of a swept surface is that it does not bend as the path curve bends. If you need it to bend, use a skinned surface.

- A skinned surface is very similar to a swept surface. The difference is that the cross section is aligned with the tangent vector

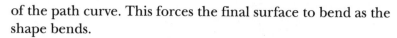

of the path curve. This forces the final surface to bend as the shape bends.

- You can create more flexible skinned and swept surfaces by introducing a third NURBS curve as the path curve. First, use the path curve to position the control points of the surface. Then, use those control points to create the actual surface.

CHAPTER 11

HIGHER-ORDER SURFACES IN DIRECTX

In this last chapter, I'd like to talk about some of the surface features that are built into DirectX. Some books might discuss these features with explanations of all of the parameters and the differences between the different types of surfaces. At this point, you already know the difference between a Bezier surface and a B-spline surface, so I'm not going to go over that again. Instead, I will go over the following topics.

- DirectX versus doing it yourself
- DirectX higher-order surfaces
- Bezier surfaces using DirectX

DirectX versus Doing It Yourself

At this point, you might be getting a sinking feeling as you begin to realize that much of the math you have just learned is actually rolled into a simple, easy to use API. This is mostly true, although I'd like to explain up front why it is still very useful to understand the math. It is true that DirectX has a higher-order surface API and it is supported by some pieces

> **NOTE**
>
> Although I don't cover it explicitly, OpenGL also has hardware and software support for higher-order surfaces. If you work with OpenGL, I would strongly recommend looking into the NURBS features.

of hardware. However, there are downsides associated with having too much work done for you.

There is a school of thought that says that you should understand everything that an API is doing before you use it. That is less true in some circumstances than in others and sometimes it becomes a religious debate that I don't really want to address. Looking at NURBS specifically, a deeper understanding of the mathematics can lead to much more effective usage of the API. For instance, many NURBS APIs take

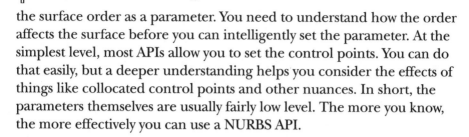

the surface order as a parameter. You need to understand how the order affects the surface before you can intelligently set the parameter. At the simplest level, most APIs allow you to set the control points. You can do that easily, but a deeper understanding helps you consider the effects of things like collocated control points and other nuances. In short, the parameters themselves are usually fairly low level. The more you know, the more effectively you can use a NURBS API.

One feature of some API calls is that they let the hardware do most of the work. You set an array of control points and the hardware creates the actual vertices. This can be very advantageous because you limit the amount of data that lives on the CPU. There is a downside to this. Imagine you have a NURBS object and you want to do collision detection. If you have the vertices, you can work with them in the collision detection calculations. Many classes could cause the "hidden" vertices to suffer. A few examples are shadow generation, picking, and collision detection.

If you needed the vertex data, but really wanted to take advantage of hardware surfaces, there is at least one way that you could have your cake and eat it too. You could send one set of control points to the card for hardware acceleration and use a second set for your calculations. This would require you to perform redundant calculations, but you could optimize the CPU calculations by remembering the fact that you don't need lighting values and other visible attributes.

> **NOTE**
>
> Each of the samples in earlier chapters recomputed the vertex buffer with every frame because of the animation. Remember, you do not need to recompute the vertices if the geometry is static.

Of course, hardware acceleration has a downside in that some people might not have the hardware. In some cases, you might want to use DirectX patches, but fall back to your own methods if the hardware isn't present.

Finally, one difference between the DirectX API and your own code is the amount of control you have over the final shape. For instance, DirectX doesn't give you low-level control over knot values and other tweaks. In some cases, you might need to render a model as a set of patches rather than one complete object.

Remember, there are pros and cons to using any tool. Depending on your needs, you might find that you can easily get by with the DirectX surface API. Hopefully, a deeper understanding of the math lets you use it better. You might also find that you absolutely need the lower level of control or some of the other features of a do-it-yourself solution. It's not my place to try to push you in either direction. I just try to give you enough information to make good decisions.

Higher-Order Surfaces in DirectX

This book will be released at roughly the same time as DirectX 9.0. Because of that, I have chosen to concentrate on DX8.1 rather than run the risk of talking about DX9 too early. Having said that, it is public knowledge that the higher-order surfaces will not be dramatically different. If you have already moved to DX9, the basic concepts of this section will remain the same, but you should read the DX9 documentation for new features.

In the near future, hardware support for higher-order surfaces will grow to the point where true NURBS or B-spline surfaces might be extremely attractive for many applications. In some cases, the hardware will support much more than simple surface tessellation. Some cards will support adaptive tessellation and displacement mapping.

DirectX supports both triangle and rectangle patches. They will be accelerated in hardware if your hardware supports them. If it does not, you can drop down to the reference device if you want to experiment with them. Both types of patches are defined by two structures, `D3DRECTPATCH_INFO` and `D3DTRIPATCH_INFO`. Both structures are defined next.

The offset values are offsets into the vertex buffer. They are explained visually in Figure 11.1.

Once these structures are created, you can render the patches with a call to `DrawRectPatch` or `DrawTriPatch`.

```
HRESULT DrawRectPatch(UINT Handle, CONST float *pNumSegs,
                      CONST D3DRECTPATCH_INFO *pRectPatchInfo);
HRESULT DrawTriPatch(UINT Handle, CONST float *pNumSegs,
                     CONST D3DRECTPATCH_INFO *pRectPatchInfo);
```

Table 11.1 D3DRECTPATCH_INFO Structure

Member	Data Type	Comments
Basis	D3DBASISTYPE	This parameter defines the type of surface. For example, DirectX 8.1 supports Bezier, B-spline, and interpolated surfaces.
Order	D3DORDERTYPE	This defines the order of the surface. You can choose linear, quadratic, cubic, and quintic. If you want to create a higher-order surface, you will probably have to do it yourself.
Width	UINT	This is the width of the control grid.
Height	UINT	This is the height of the control grid.
Stride	UINT	This is the number of vertices between successive rows of control points. In most cases, this value will be equal to the width value.
StartVertex OffsetWidth	UINT	This is the offset to the first vertex as shown in Figure 11.1.
StartVertex OffsetHeight	UINT	This is the vertical offset to the first vertex as shown in Figure 11.1.

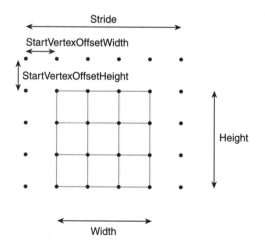

Figure 11.1 *Vertex layout for rectangular patches.*

Table 11.2   D3DTRIPATCH_INFO Structure

Member	Data Type	Comments
Basis	D3DBASISTYPE	This parameter defines the type of surface. For example, DirectX 8.1 supports Bezier, B-spline, and interpolated surfaces.
Order	D3DORDERTYPE	This defines the order of the surface. You can choose linear, quadratic, cubic, and quintic. If you want to create a higher-order surface, you will probably have to do it yourself.
NumVertices	UINT	This is the number of vertices in the triangle patch.
StartVertex Offset	UINT	This is the offset to the first vertex in the patch.

The Handle parameter of each of these functions provides a mechanism to deal with cached patches. If a patch is dynamic, it is best to call these functions with a handle value of 0. This tells the device not to cache the resulting patch. If the patch is static, you can call the function with a non-zero handle value. The next time you want to draw the same patch, call the function with the same handle value, but specify NULL for the last parameter. This will tell the device to use the cached patch.

The pNumSegs parameter specifies the number of segments in each side of the patch. In the case of rectangle patches, this parameter should be a pointer to a set of four floats. In the case of triangle patches, it should point to three floats. This gives you some control over how the patch is tessellated. Alternatively, you could specify NULL for this parameter and set the D3DRS_PATCHSEGMENTS render state.

These functions will obtain their control points from the current stream source. The current source should be a vertex buffer created with the D3DUSAGE_RTPATCHES flag. This tells the device that the vertices will be used to generate patches. The vertex structure is very simple. You only need to specify the position because everything else will be generated for you.

```
struct PATCH_VERTEX
{
        float x, y, z;
};
```

Finally, you must tell the device to generate the proper normal vectors if you want any lighting effects. You can do this by creating a custom vertex shader based on a special vertex declaration. The declaration below tells the device that it must generate vertex normals in addition to vertex positions.

```
DWORD Declaration[] =
{
        D3DVSD_STREAM(0),
        D3DVSD_REG(D3DVSDE_POSITION, D3DVSDT_FLOAT3),
        D3DVSD_STREAM_TESS(),
        D3DVSD_TESSNORMAL(D3DVSDE_POSITION, D3DVSDE_NORMAL),
        D3DVSD_END()
};
```

If you want, you can also create custom vertex shader code. In this case, I want to use this custom declaration, but I am only interested in the standard fixed-function pipeline. I can create a fixed-function shader that uses a custom declaration with the following line of code. This generates a shader handle that can be used when rendering the patches.

> **NOTE**
>
> Tesselation can also apply to texture coordinates and other vertex attributes. See the documentation for a full explanation.

```
m_pD3DDevice->CreateVertexShader(Declaration, NULL, &m_ShaderHandle, 0);
```

You now have all the basic pieces needed to generate a patch: the information needed to define a patch, a function that can draw one, and the vertex specification. Now, I'll show you how to put it all together.

Drawing a Bezier Patch with DirectX

The code for this example can be found on the CD in the \Code\ Chapter11 - DX8 Bezier Patches directory. As in previous chapters, I'm introducing the new concepts with Bezier patches simply because they are the least complex. I will walk you through a very simple application that will use DirectX to reproduce the sample you saw in Chapter 7, "Basic Surface Concepts and Bezier Surfaces."

If you look at the code, the first thing you'll notice is that there is much less of it than in previous chapters. This is because DirectX does the math for you. You no longer need to keep track of basis functions and so on. In fact, the class definition is much simpler, as shown next. The code is from BezierPatchApplication.h.

```
class CBezierPatchApplication : public CPatchApplication
{
public:
        CBezierPatchApplication();
        virtual ~CBezierPatchApplication();
```

I have kept the function names the same for consistency, but FillPatchBuffer does much less work now. The only thing you need to do is set the control vertex positions.

```
        BOOL FillPatchBuffer();

        virtual BOOL PostInitialize();
        virtual BOOL PreTerminate();
        virtual void Render();
```

There are also far fewer member variables. The index buffer is gone because DirectX handles that. The arrays of basis values are gone as well. You are left with a vertex buffer that holds the control point locations, a structure that defines the patch, and a shader handle.

```
        LPDIRECT3DVERTEXBUFFER8 m_pPatchVertices;
        D3DRECTPATCH_INFO       m_PatchInfo;
        DWORD                   m_ShaderHandle;
};
```

The implementation is also much simpler, as you will see when you look at BezierPatchApplication.cpp. The first thing you'll notice is that I have defined the vertex buffer size so that it only holds the control points. In this case, I am creating a 4x4 Bezier patch.

```
#define NUM_U_POINTS 4
#define NUM_V_POINTS 4
#define NUM_TOTAL_VERTICES (NUM_U_POINTS * NUM_V_POINTS)
```

The PostInitialize function does less, but it does some new things. In addition to setting up the vertex buffer, I have also enabled real DirectX lighting because you don't have direct access to the vertex color. You could still program your own lighting in a vertex shader, but that is not covered here.

```
BOOL CBezierPatchApplication::PostInitialize()
{
        CPatchApplication::PostInitialize();
```

The call to CreateVertexBuffer has several subtle changes. First, the number of vertices is much smaller (16 in this case). Also, the vertices are set up to be patch vertices in addition to being dynamic. Finally, the vertex format is now limited to the position, as shown in the previous section.

```
        if (FAILED(m_pD3DDevice->CreateVertexBuffer(
                        NUM_TOTAL_VERTICES * sizeof(PATCH_VERTEX),
                        D3DUSAGE_RTPATCHES | D3DUSAGE_DYNAMIC,
                        D3DFVF_PATCHVERTEX, D3DPOOL_DEFAULT,
                        &m_pPatchVertices)))
                return FALSE;
```

Next, I set up the patch info structure. I'm doing it once in PostInitialize because it never changes. If you decide to change it dynamically, you'll have to move this code to the Render function. This structure specifies a 4x4 cubic Bezier patch. I don't have to worry about the offset values because the vertex buffer only contains vertices for this one patch.

```
        m_PatchInfo.StartVertexOffsetWidth  = 0;
        m_PatchInfo.StartVertexOffsetHeight = 0;
        m_PatchInfo.Width  = NUM_U_POINTS;
        m_PatchInfo.Height = NUM_V_POINTS;
        m_PatchInfo.Stride = NUM_U_POINTS;
```

```
m_PatchInfo.Basis  = D3DBASIS_BEZIER;
m_PatchInfo.Order  = D3DORDER_CUBIC;
```

The following code is the most significant departure from the earlier samples. In the earlier samples, I wanted to limit the DirectX specificity as much as possible, so I avoided DirectX lights. That is unavoidable now that I don't have direct access to the vertex colors in the final patch. In light of that, the following code enables shading that will be calculated by DirectX. This requires a light and a material. To keep things simple, I create a white directional light and a white material. The net result will be exactly the same as the lighting calculations done in the previous chapter.

```
D3DLIGHT8 Light;
D3DMATERIAL8 Material;
memset(&Light, 0, sizeof(D3DLIGHT8));
memset(&Material, 0, sizeof(D3DMATERIAL8));

Light.Type       = D3DLIGHT_DIRECTIONAL;
Light.Diffuse.r = Light.Diffuse.g = Light.Diffuse.b = 1.0f;
Light.Direction = D3DXVECTOR3(0.0f, -1.0f, 0.0f);
m_pD3DDevice->SetLight(0, &Light);
m_pD3DDevice->LightEnable(0, TRUE);

Material.Diffuse = Light.Diffuse;
m_pD3DDevice->SetMaterial(&Material);
```

Next, I need to set up a fixed-function vertex shader with a custom declaration as discussed earlier. The following declaration tells the device to generate a patch based on the information found in stream 0. It also tells the device to tessellate the normals of the patch vertices based on the same control points. The actual computations will also be based on the parameters of the patch info structure.

```
DWORD Declaration[] =
{
        D3DVSD_STREAM(0),
        D3DVSD_REG(D3DVSDE_POSITION, D3DVSDT_FLOAT3),
        D3DVSD_STREAM_TESS(),
        D3DVSD_TESSNORMAL(D3DVSDE_POSITION, D3DVSDE_NORMAL),
        D3DVSD_END()
};
```

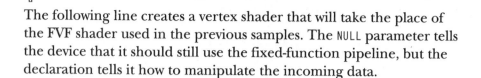

The following line creates a vertex shader that will take the place of the FVF shader used in the previous samples. The NULL parameter tells the device that it should still use the fixed-function pipeline, but the declaration tells it how to manipulate the incoming data.

```
m_pD3DDevice->CreateVertexShader(Declaration, NULL,
&m_ShaderHandle, 0);

    return TRUE;
}
```

Sadly, the magic is gone from FillPatchBuffer. The function no longer needs to compute patch values. Instead, it simply locks the vertex buffer, sets the control point positions, and unlocks the buffer. It's now so simple that I have chosen not to include the code in the text.

The real work is done by the device in response to a call to DrawRectPatch. This happens in the Render function.

```
void CBezierPatchApplication::Render()
{
    CPatchApplication::Render();
```

Before you render, you need to enable lighting. The light itself was set up in PostInitialize, but you still need to enable the render state. The reason this is done every frame is that the underlying framework does not use lighting when rendering the background grid. The second call to SetRenderState ensures that the normal vectors are all normalized before they are fed into the lighting calculations. If they are not normalized, the lighting calculations will not yield the correct results.

```
m_pD3DDevice->SetRenderState(D3DRS_LIGHTING, TRUE);
m_pD3DDevice->SetRenderState(D3DRS_NORMALIZENORMALS, TRUE);
```

A call to FillPatchBuffer updates the control point positions. Remember, you would not need to do this every frame if the mesh was static.

```
FillPatchBuffer();
```

The following lines do the setup for the patch itself. In this case, I have set the number of segments for each side to the same value of 8.0. I would encourage you to experiment with different values and different combinations to see how these values affect the final result. Also, the actual source code has a wireframe mode that you can easily enable. You will be able to see the effects more clearly if you switch to a wireframe fill mode.

```
float NumSegments[4];
NumSegments[0] = NumSegments[1] = NumSegments[2] =
NumSegments[3] = 8.0f;
```

In addition to setting the stream source, I also need to set the shader handle. In the previous samples, I didn't need to do this because the framework vertices and the patch vertices shared the same FVF. This is no longer the case. Also, remember that the vertex buffer only contains control point positions.

```
m_pD3DDevice->SetVertexShader(m_ShaderHandle);
m_pD3DDevice->SetStreamSource(0, m_pPatchVertices,
sizeof(PATCH_VERTEX));
```

Now it's time to draw the actual patch. I use handle 0 because FillPatchBuffer changes the vertices every frame. There is no advantage to caching anything. The patch itself is defined by the patch info structure and the vertices in stream 0.

```
m_pD3DDevice->DrawRectPatch(0, NumSegments, &m_PatchInfo);
```

Finally, I disable lighting. This is done because the underlying framework does not use lighting. In other situations, you probably don't need to toggle this state in every frame.

```
m_pD3DDevice->SetRenderState(D3DRS_LIGHTING, FALSE);
}
```

Figure 11.2 shows a screenshot from this application. As you can see, the results are very similar to Figure 7.11, but with far less code. If your hardware accelerates patches, the application probably also runs faster.

Figure 11.3 shows a wireframe view. In this case, I have set the sides to have 1, 2, 3, and 4 segments. The control points are the same.

In Conclusion...

You have just seen how you can render patches very simply using DirectX. The simplicity might make DirectX patches very attractive, but hardware acceleration can be a double-edged sword. I envision most projects falling into one of three categories. You might be able to use DirectX all the time, you might not be able to use it at all, or you might want to use it for rendering, but do your own calculations for physics, legacy support, or some other reason.

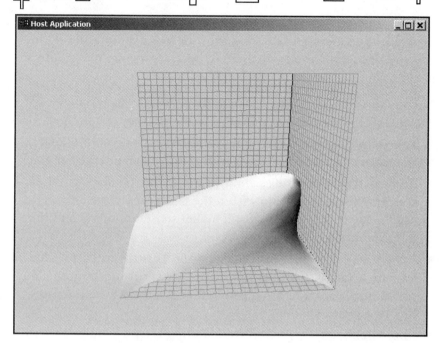

Figure 11.2 *DirectX Bezier Patch.*

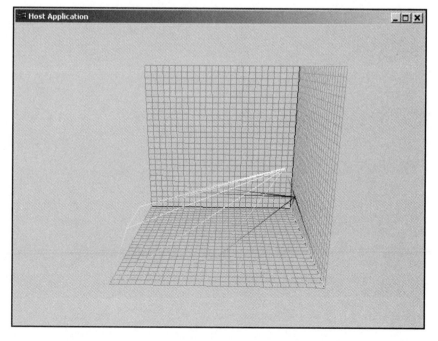

Figure 11.3 *Wireframe with different segment counts per side.*

In any case, remember that you have several tools available to you. You should always spend time evaluating your tools and choose the right one for the right job. When you do that, here are a couple of points to remember.

- DirectX offers hardware support for rectangle and triangle patches. If the user has the right hardware, they can be very fast.

- The DirectX patches offer you simplicity at the cost of control. You must evaluate your needs to see if they make sense for you.

- The patch info structures allow you to define patches based on concepts you already know from the earlier text. Even if you do use the DirectX solution, it still makes sense to understand the different orders and basis types.

- In addition to the position calculations, DirectX will also calculate the normals if you set up the proper vertex declaration. You can control vertex lighting with either the fixed-function pipeline or a vertex shader.

- I have deliberately ignored changes that are present in DirectX 9.0 or OpenGL. Make sure you check the documentation to see how surfaces are supported in other APIs.

PART FOUR

APPENDIXES

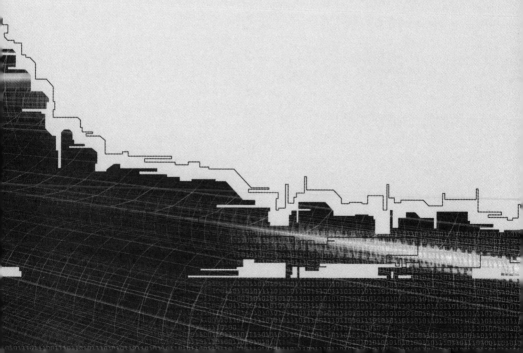

APPENDIX A

DERIVATIVE CALCULUS

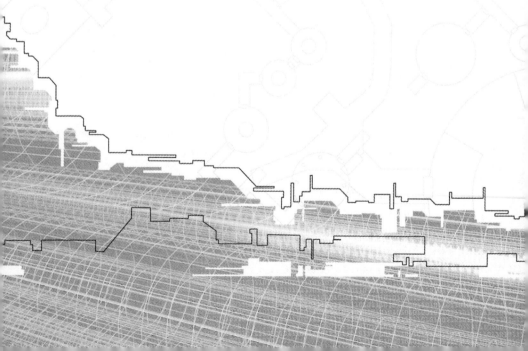

M ost people learn calculus either at the end of high school or the beginning of college. As a result, most people believe that calculus is a difficult topic. My personal belief is that a great deal of the difficulty comes from how the topic is taught. Most math classes concentrate on the mathematics of calculus without showing much in the way of practical application. In this appendix, I want to briefly explain one of the two branches of calculus in a way that most people will be able to understand. I explain the applications of calculus in the chapters themselves. If you already know calculus, you may notice that this appendix is not a complete discussion, but I do cover the following important concepts:

- What is differential calculus?
- What is a derivative?
- Computing derivatives of polynomial functions
- Computing derivatives of trigonometric functions
- Computing partial derivatives of multivariable functions

What Is Differential Calculus?

There are two branches of calculus: differential calculus and integral calculus. *Integral* calculus is a method used to determine the area under the curve of a given function. Most of the time, it isn't useful to think of this as a literal computation of area. Instead, it is useful for determining how the results of a function accumulate with respect to a given variable. Integral calculus is used to answer questions like the one shown graphically in Figure A.1.

There is also *differential* calculus, which is a method used to determine how the value of a given function changes with respect to a given variable. In basic terms, this is the slope of a function at a certain point along the curve. Differential calculus is used to answer questions like the one shown in Figure A.2.

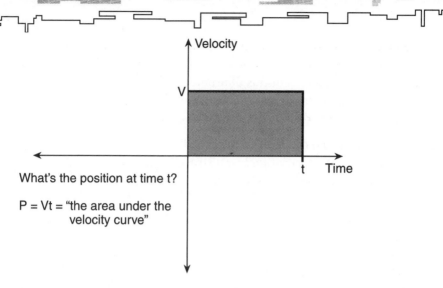

What's the position at time t?

P = Vt = "the area under the velocity curve"

Figure A.1 *An example of where integral calculus is useful.*

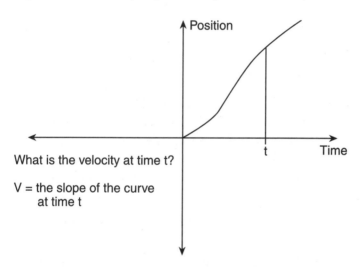

What is the velocity at time t?

V = the slope of the curve at time t

Figure A.2 *An example of where differential calculus is useful.*

In this appendix, I will only talk about differential calculus because you need it to compute the slopes of curves and the normals of surfaces. I talk briefly about integral calculus in some of the chapters.

What Is a Derivative?

Differential calculus is used to determine the derivative of a function. A derivative of the function **F** is another function that describes how the value of **F** changes with respect to some variable. Most of the examples in this appendix feature functions of **x**, so most functions are denoted as **F(x)**. The derivative of a function is denoted as **dF(x)/dx**. In plain language, this is read as "the change in **F(x)** with respect to **x**". Similarly, you could talk about **dy/dx**, **dz/dx**, **dz/dy**, and many other derivatives.

So, a derivative basically describes the rate of change of the output with respect to the input variable. For a straight line, this rate of change is the slope and it is the same for every point on the line. That isn't the case for other functions. Consider Figure A.3.

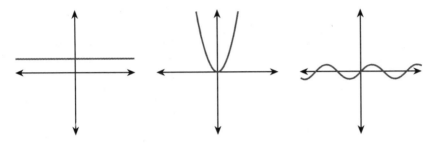

Figure A.3   *Functions and how they change.*

In the leftmost graph, the curve is a straight line. The change in y with respect to x is equal at all points along the curve. In the center graph, the change of **y** with respect to **x** is different at all three of the designated points. In fact, it is different for all points along the curve. The rightmost graph shows a sine wave. The value of **y** is periodic and the rate of change in **y** is also periodic.

Several chapters demonstrate the value of knowing how variables change with respect to each other. It is not enough to know that they change. You need a way to derive the equation that describes how they change. That is the purpose of the derivative. Before I get into the real math, get out a piece of paper and a pencil and graph out some rough approximations of how the slopes change in each of the graphs in Figure A.3. You should get something that looks like the rough sketches in Figure A.4.

The next sections describe how to find the actual equations for these functions. These derivates are used frequently in this book.

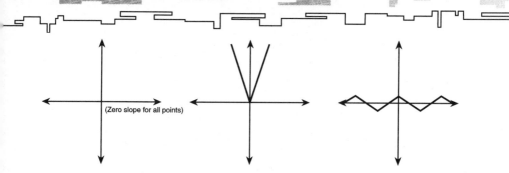

Figure A.4   *Graph of the slopes from Figure A.3.*

Derivatives of Polynomial Functions

Recall that a polynomial function is one that takes the form shown in Equation A.1—where the *order* of the function is the value of the largest exponent.

$$y = C_0 x^N + C_1 x^{N-1} + C_2 x^{N-2} + \ldots + C_N x^0$$

Equation A.I   *The form of a polynomial function.*

Note that the values of any of the coefficients can be zero. A line is a very simple polynomial in the form shown next.

$$y = ax + b$$

Equation A.2   *The equation for a line.*

For a line, the change in **y** with respect to **x** is just the slope, which can be computed with the simple "rise over run" equation as shown in Figure A.5.

If you know how to compute the slope of a line, you know how to compute the derivative of that line for any value of **x**. Congratulations, you know a little bit of calculus. However, this obviously doesn't extend to higher-order polynomials like the one shown in Figure A.6. Figure A.6 shows that you can't just pick two points on a curve and compute the correct slope at any given point.

Still, Figure A.6 reveals the first hint about how you can compute the slope at a certain point. You can think of line AB in the figure as an

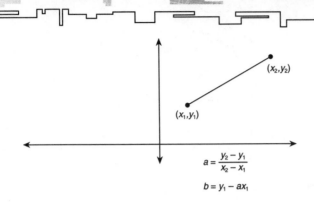

Figure A.5   *Computing the slope of a line.*

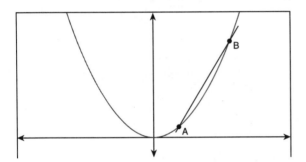

Figure A.6   *The slope on a higher-order polynomial.*

approximation of the slope at point A. The closer the two points are, the closer the approximate slope is to the correct slope. With that in mind, you can redraw Figure A.6 as Figure A.7.

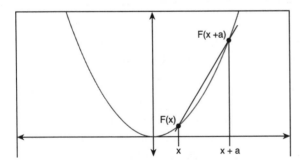

Figure A.7   *Reformulating the approximate slope.*

Based on Figure A.7 and the equations in Figure A.5, you can say that the approximate slope becomes more and more correct as **a** approaches zero. Mathematicians write this in the form shown in Equation A.3.

$$slope = \frac{dF(x)}{dx} = \lim_{a \to 0} \frac{F(x+a) - F(x)}{a}$$

Equation A.3   *The derivative of a function expressed as a limit.*

Here I have introduced the concept of a *limit*. There are many rules that affect how limits work, but you don't need to know most of them, so I won't explain them here. For simple polynomial functions, the rules are pretty straightforward. Consider Equation A.4 as an example of how the limit applies to a simple polynomial.

$$f(x) = x^2$$

$$\frac{dF(x)}{dx} = \lim_{a \to 0} \frac{F(x+a) - F(x)}{a} = \lim_{a \to 0} \frac{x^2 + 2ax + a^2 - x^2}{a} = \lim_{a \to 0} 2x + a = 2x$$

$$\frac{dF(x)}{dx} = 2x$$

Equation A.4   *The derivative of a simple polynomial.*

As you can see, you compute the limit by setting **a** equal to 0. It may look like you need to divide by 0, but it works out such that you can cancel out **a** without dealing with the problems associated with dividing by 0. Equation A.4 shows the general operations that will apply to any simple polynomial. I will leave it to you to work out examples of higher-order functions. Keep in mind that I have not given you sufficient information to compute the derivative of Equation A.5. That requires much more information and doesn't really apply to any problems in this book.

$$F(x) = \frac{\sqrt{x^5 + 1}}{\sqrt{x}}$$

$$\frac{dF(x)}{dx} = ???$$

Equation A.5   *I haven't told you how to solve this!*

If you have taken the time to experiment with some simple higher-order polynomials, you will find that each of their derivatives adhere to the following form.

$$\frac{d(x^N)}{dx} = Nx^{N-1}$$

Equation A.6   *Basic derivative of a simple polynomial.*

You may have also noticed that the derivative of sums is the sum of derivatives, meaning that you can break an equation apart, compute the simple derivatives, and add the resulting derivatives back together. This is shown in Equation A.7.

$$\frac{d(F(x) + G(x))}{dx} = \frac{dF(x)}{dx} + \frac{dG(x)}{dx}$$

Equation A.7   *The derivative of a sum.*

You now have everything you need to compute the derivatives of the polynomials you'll find in most of the chapters of this book. Figure A.8 shows some examples. The top row is a series of polynomials and the bottom row shows the graphs of their derivatives.

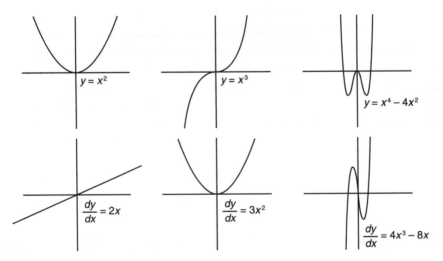

Figure A.8   *Derivatives of polynomial functions.*

Nearly all of the functions in this book can be expressed as some form of polynomial and in almost all cases it is advantageous to know how to compute the slope along a curve or surface. You now have the basic tools you need to compute those slopes. The explanations here are general and abstract, but you will see concrete uses of these concepts in nearly every chapter.

The Quotient Rule

NURBS are a form of curves and surfaces that are expressed quotients (fractions). When you want to find the slope on a NURBS curve, you need a way of finding the derivative of a quotient. There is a simple rule that can be applied when differentiating quotients, which is appropriately called "the quotient rule." You can express the numerator and denominator as separate functions, find the derivatives of each, and then put them together as shown in Equation A.8.

$$\frac{d}{dx}\left(\frac{f(x)}{g(x)}\right) = \frac{g(x)\dfrac{df(x)}{dx} - f(x)\dfrac{dg(x)}{dx}}{(g(x))^2}$$

Equation A.8   *The quotient rule.*

The quotients shown in this book are relatively straightforward. Both the numerator and denominator are simple polynomials. Although the results are sometimes ugly, the quotient rule gives you a useful and straightforward tool to divide and conquer quotients.

Derivatives of Trigonometric Functions

Most of the curves and surfaces in this book are based on polynomial functions, but trigonometric functions are also very interesting because of their periodicity. You can also find the slope of a trigonometric function with a derivative. Understanding exactly how the derivative works is a little bit more involved, so I encourage you to start out by plotting a sine wave and then plotting out the slopes at points along that wave. Your graph should look something like Figure A.9.

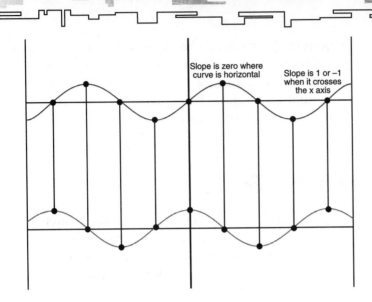

Figure A.9   *Approximating the derivative of a sine wave.*

At this point, you might notice that this looks a lot like a cosine wave. If you repeat the exercise with a cosine, you should see something like Figure A.10.

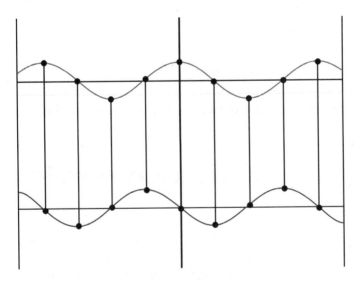

Figure A.10   *Approximating the derivative of a cosine wave.*

This looks a lot like a negative sine wave. Now, you might say that you have "proven by inspection" that the derivatives of sine and cosine are what you see in Equation A.9.

$$\frac{d(\sin(x))}{dx} = \cos(x)$$

$$\frac{d(\cos(x))}{dx} = -\sin(x)$$

Equation A.9   *The derivatives of trigonometric functions.*

The derivatives shown in Equation A.9 are true, but they lack any sort of mathematical rigor. In a math class, you'd need to be able to show why this is true. Recall that one way of approximating sine and cosine is with a Taylor series as shown in Equation A.10.

$$\sin(x) = x - \frac{x^3}{3!} + \frac{x^5}{5!} - \frac{x^7}{7!} + \ldots$$

$$\cos(x) = 1 - \frac{x^2}{2!} + \frac{x^4}{4!} - \frac{x^6}{6!} + \ldots$$

Equation A.10   *Taylor series approximations for sine and cosine.*

Wait a second! You know how to compute derivatives of polynomials and a Taylor series is just a big polynomial. You can compute the derivatives of sine and cosine by finding the derivatives of their Taylor series as shown in Equation A.11.

$$\frac{d(\sin(x))}{dx} = 1 - \frac{3x^2}{3!} + \frac{5x^4}{5!} - \ldots = 1 - \frac{x^2}{2!} + \frac{x^4}{4!} + \ldots = \cos(x)$$

$$\frac{d(\cos(x))}{dx} = 0 - \frac{2x}{2!} + \frac{4x^3}{4!} - \ldots = -x + \frac{x^3}{3!} - \ldots = -\left(x - \frac{x^3}{3!} + \ldots\right) = -\sin(x)$$

Equation A.11   *The derivatives of sine and cosine via the Taylor series.*

So, the graphs in Figures A.9 and A.10 were correct. But then again, you knew that.

I am only covering sine and cosine here because I only really use those two functions in the book. Remember that there are derivatives for tangent, secant, and even the dreaded hyperbolic cosecant. Most calculus textbooks include a table of derivatives of common functions. A textbook is the best place to learn more about how these derivatives are computed.

Partial Derivatives of Multivariable Functions

Most curves are functions of one variable, but surfaces and other functions can involve many variables. For surfaces, you might express the y coordinate as a function of the x and z coordinates, as shown in Equation A.12.

$$y = x^2 + xz + z^2$$

Equation A.12   *y as a function of x and z.*

In many cases, you will need to compute the *partial derivative*, which is the derivative with respect to only one of the two variables. In a general math class, this can become a bit complicated. You can safely compute partial derivatives fairly easily for most of the applications in this book. When computing the partial derivative of a multivariable polynomial, choose which variable you want to find the derivative for and treat the others as constants. Then, compute the derivative as you did for simple polynomials. Repeat for all the variables as needed. Equation A.13 shows an example of this.

$$y = x^2 + xz + z^2$$

$$\frac{dy}{dx} = 2x + z$$

$$\frac{dy}{dz} = x + 2z$$

Equation A.13   *A more complicated partial derivative.*

This is not a general approach for all equations. I haven't given you enough information to solve Equation A.14 (and many others).

$$y = x + \cos(xz) + z^2$$

Equation A.14 *A more complicated multivariable polynomial.*

The examples in this book do not involve this kind of equation, and I want to stress the point that I am giving you only what you need in this book.

Caveats and Conclusions

As you use these rules, remember that I am only skimming the surface of what you can do with calculus. These rules will help you with the examples in this book. I hope that the chapters give you a solid feel for what these equations actually mean. If the equations in this appendix don't make sense, start sketching out curves and slopes and looking at the resulting numbers. You will probably get a feel for it much more quickly.

Personally, I had a better understanding of calculus once it was put into physical terms. I talk about velocity, acceleration, and other physical concepts in many of the chapters. You may find these equations easier to understand when you think of them in those terms.

In this appendix, I have presented a couple of equations that don't fit the simple rules I've laid out. You shouldn't encounter many of these forms in this book, but you might in other areas. If you do, remember Equation A.3. In the worst case, you can solve the equation for two very close points along the curve and approximate the slope using Equation A.2. In many cases, you will be computing positions in order to populate vertex data. You can derive approximate slope values from those positions. If you find yourself trying to solve these complex equations often, invest in a calculus book.

APPENDIX B

A Quick Look at Vectors

M ost graphics books concentrate heavily on vectors because they form the basis of nearly everything that is moved and drawn on the screen. In this book, very little material depends on vectors (although they do rear their ugly little heads occasionally). The only place you really need to worry about vector operations is when you are computing the normal vectors for a surface. I'm including this appendix to make sure we are all on the same page about the following concepts:

- A simple definition of vectors
- Normalizing vectors
- Computing the vector cross product

What Is a Vector?

A vector, in the simplest terms, is a set of numbers that describe a position or direction somewhere in a given coordinate system. Note that vectors are different from *scalars*, which are numbers that represent only a single value or magnitude. For instance, 60mph is a scalar value, but 60mph heading north can be thought of as a vector. Most of the vectors you will deal with in this book are properties of the curves and surfaces themselves. For instance, you will frequently deal with the slope of a curve or the normal vector to a specific point on a surface.

Normalizing Vectors

Vectors contain both magnitude (length) and direction. However, in some cases it's useful to separate one from the other. You may want to know just the length, or you may want to work with the direction as a *normalized unit vector*—a vector with a length of one, but the same direction. To compute the magnitude of a vector, simply apply the Pythagorean theorem.

$$|V| = |(X,Y,Z)| = \sqrt{(X^2 + Y^2 + Z^2)}$$

Once you compute the magnitude, the normalized unit vector can be found by dividing each component by the magnitude.

$$N = (\frac{X}{|V|}, \frac{Y}{|V|}, \frac{Z}{|V|})$$

Most surface normal vectors should be normalized to ensure that lighting calculations yield the correct results.

Vector Cross Product

The cross product of two vectors is the most common vector operation in the second half of this book. Computing the cross product of two vectors gives you a third vector that is perpendicular to both of the original vectors. To visualize this, imagine three points in space as in Figure B.1. Mathematically speaking, those three points define a plane for which there is only one perpendicular "up direction". Using those three points, we can get two vectors, V_{ab} and V_{ac}. The cross product of those two vectors is perpendicular to the two vectors and is therefore perpendicular to the plane.

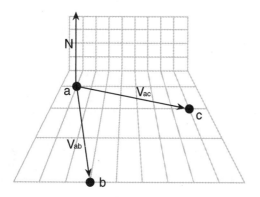

Figure B.1   *The cross product of two vectors.*

The cross product of two vectors is computed as follows:

$$U \times V = N = (X_n, Y_n, Z_n)$$

$$X_n = (Y_u * Z_v) - (Z_u * Y_v)$$
$$Y_n = (Z_u * X_v) - (X_u * Z_v)$$
$$Z_n = (X_u * Y_v) - (Y_u * X_v)$$

It is important to note here that the vector N is perpendicular to the two vectors, but it is not necessarily a unit vector. You may need to normalize N to obtain a unit vector. This is the easiest way to find the vector that is perpendicular to a surface—something very necessary in lighting and shading calculations. It is also important to note that the cross product is not commutative. Changing the order of operations changes the sign of the cross product.

$U \times V = -(V \times U)$

When you are computing surface normals, you may find that the wrong side of the surface is being lit. If this is the case, you've probably computed the cross product in the wrong order. Whenever your lighting doesn't look right, double-check your cross products before you start dissecting other parts of your code.

In Conclusion...

Compared to most other books, this book doesn't rely very much on vector math. This appendix contains only the most cursory information. For this book, you can get by with the four main points listed next.

- Vectors represent positions, orientations, and directions in multidimensional space.
- The magnitudes of vectors can be computed using the Pythagorean theorem.
- Vectors can be normalized into unit vectors describing their direction.
- The vector cross product is a normal vector that is perpendicular to both vectors.

APPENDIX C

BIBLIOGRAPHY

I have included references for a small sampling of texts and Web sites available for further information. There are many excellent resources available, but I have chosen this handful based on their accessibility to someone without an advanced mathematical background. Each one of these references would make an excellent source of more information should you choose to explore this topic further.

Books

An Introduction to NURBS: With Historical Perspective
David F. Rogers
More information about this book can be found at:
http://www.amazon.com/exec/obidos/ASIN/1558606696

The NURBS Book (Monographs in Visual Communications)
Les Piegl and Wayne Tiller
More information about this book can be found at:
http://www.amazon.com/exec/obidos/tg/detail/-/3540615458/

3D Game Engine Design: A Practical Approach to Real-Time Computer Graphics
David H. Eberly
More information about this book can be found at:
http://www.amazon.com/exec/obidos/ASIN/1558605932/

Web Sites

Eric Weisstein's World of Mathematics (MathWorld)
http://mathworld.wolfram.com/

Gamasutra (A game developer site with many useful articles)
http://www.gamasutra.com/

GameDev.net (Another site with useful resources)
http://www.gamedev.net/

Google (Most searches on terms like "knot vector" will produce good results)
http://www.google.com/

APPENDIX D

WHAT'S ON THE CD

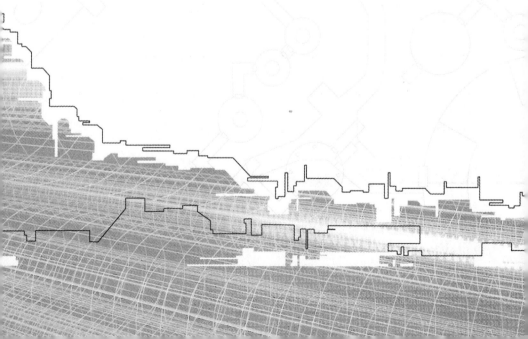

I n addition to the source code, the CD includes a few useful and interesting applications. Each includes its own installer and instructions and I recommend at least taking a look at each of them. Below are short descriptions of each.

The DirectX 8.1 SDK

Chances are, you already have this, but it is included in case you don't. In either case, take a look at the curve and surface features that are included in the DirectX SDK. The documentation talks about them, but the material in this book should give you a better sense of what the features and parameters actually do.

Rhino 2.0 (Evaluation Version)

Rhinoceros is a NURBS-based modeler that employs many of the techniques shown in this book. It can be useful for several reasons. You can use it as a NURBS modeler and export the results in a polygonal format. More advanced readers could also consider downloading the Rhino I/O toolkit and writing code to read NURBS files natively. This could create many possibilities for taking advantage of NURBS features within your game engine. Finally, even if you don't care about that, it might be interesting to take a look at Rhino to see how a NURBS modeler really works. I showed you many techniques in the samples, but Rhino has many more features.

Xfrog (Evaluation Version)

Xfrog is a very interesting plant modeling tool. I have included this software because it is a great example of how you can create interesting shapes and animations once you begin to think in terms of parameters. In some of the later examples (such as the spring model), I stressed the advantages of thinking in terms of parametric objects. Although many of the Xfrog features are not NURBS-based, nearly all of them feature some form of parametric control. You will find that you can create some amazing shapes and animations with this tool. Graphics cards are beginning to be fast enough that you can consider filling your game worlds with these lifelike plants.

Index

www.xfrog.com

GAME DEVELOPMENT.
IT'S SERIOUS BUSINESS.

"Game programming is without a doubt the most intellectually challenging field of Computer Science in the world. However, we would be fooling ourselves if we said that we are 'serious' people! Writing (and reading) a game programming book should be an exciting adventure for both the author and the reader."

—André LaMothe,
Series Editor

Gamedev.net

The most comprehensive game development resource

The latest news in game development
The most active forums and chatrooms anywhere, with
insights and tips from experienced game developers
Links to thousands of additional game development resources
Thorough book and product reviews
Over 1000 game development articles!
Game design
Graphics
DirectX
OpenGL
AI
Art
Music
Physics
Source Code
Sound
Assembly
And More!

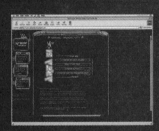